English in Fact

Students' Book

Michael Lucas

Heinemann Educational Books

Heinemann Educational Books Ltd
22 Bedford Square, London WC1B 3HH

LONDON   EDINBURGH   MELBOURNE   AUCKLAND
HONG KONG   SINGAPORE   KUALA LUMPUR   NEW DELHI
IBADAN   NAIROBI   JOHANNESBURG   EXETER (NH)
KINGSTON   PORT OF SPAIN

English in Fact is published with an accompanying
Teachers' Book (ISBN 0 435 28421 5)

 British Library Cataloguing in Publication Data

Lucas, Michael Arthur
   English in fact.
   Students' book
   1. English language – Composition and exercises
   I. Title
   428   PE1112

   ISBN 0-435-28420-7

Cover design by Jon Allen
Line illustrations by Oxford Illustrators

Set in 11/13pt Times by Filmtype Services Limited,
Scarborough
Printed and bound in Great Britain by
Spottiswoode Ballantyne Limited, Colchester and
London

Acknowledgements

While every effort has been made to trace the owners of copyright material in this book, there have been one or two cases where the author and publishers have been unable to find the sources. We should be grateful to hear from anyone who recognises their copyright material and is unacknowledged. We shall be pleased to make the necessary corrections in future editions of this book.

The author and publishers wish to thank the following for permission to reproduce their source material and for providing technical information and photographs:

p.10 New Scientist, London

p.11 Shell U.K. Ltd (A Shell Photograph)

p.18 New Scientist, London

p.19 Lockheed Corporation

p.22 From The Observer, London

p.24 C.G. Hervey-Murray at RHM Arable Services Ltd

p.28 United Nations

p.30 New Scientist, London

p.34 The Royal Navy

p.35 Lieutenant Commander D.A. Bartlett, Royal Navy

p.38 The Royal Navy

p.40 The Ministry of Defence

p.44 The Trustees of the British Museum

p.54 New Scientist, London

p.58 New Scientist, London

p.59 UNESCO/Zevaco

p.66 New Scientist, London

p.78 New Scientist, London

p.79 Australian Information Service

p.83 The Science Museum, London

CONTENTS

Introduction

English In Fact has been written for intermediate and advanced students of English as a foreign or second language who need further practice in reading descriptive texts, extracting information from them, organising this information in a systematic way and writing similar texts themselves.

English In Fact is designed for students following an academic course of study overseas who need to improve their *reading skills* in English in relation to scientific and technical texts.

English In Fact also provides relevant practice for students in the United Kingdom who are preparing specifically for the *Joint Matriculation Board (JMB) Test in English (Overseas)*.

THE UNITS

There are twenty-one units in **English In Fact**, each of which consists of a text followed by a set of exercises based on the text. The units are graded in order of difficulty both as regards the length and complexity of the text itself and the demands made on the student in the exercises which follow the text.

THE TEXTS

The texts in **English In Fact** are descriptive, in the sense that they describe processes or ideas, and are taken from a wide range of sciences, technologies and other branches of human knowledge. Texts have been chosen that will be of interest in themselves whether or not the subject of the text is directly related to the students' own area of study, and no specialist technical or scientific knowledge is assumed.

THE EXERCISES

Reference can often cause problems when reading scientific or technical texts. The purpose of the *reference* exercises is to focus on pronouns, such as 'it', 'they', 'this', 'that', and to identify what is being referred to in the text. In most cases, what is being referred to will precede the pronoun and will be a complete phrase and not a single word. For example, in Unit One 'they' (line 4) refers to the complete phrase, 'the ends of the pipelines', and not to 'ends' or 'pipelines' alone. In some cases, however, the pronoun will refer forward to something that is about to be stated. For example, in Unit One 'it' (line 17) refers to '(the fact that) nobody has ever thought of it before'. In the *vocabulary* exercises, the student is not expected to find a word or phrase in the text which means the same as the one in the exercise. Instead the student is required to find a word or phrase in the text which could be replaced by the one in the exercise. In this way it can be shown how the meaning of a word or phrase depends on its context, or where the word or phrase appears and how it is used.

The *understanding* exercises, which practise and develop the ability to extract information from a text, usually involve a set of sentences based on the text that has been read. In some exercises students are asked to judge which sentences are true and which are false according to the text. In other exercises students have to select sentences which relate to a particular aspect of the text, or arrange true sentences in the correct order. As with all exercises, it is important to read the instructions very carefully.

The *transfer* exercises may be unfamiliar to some students. These exercises practise a skill which students of all disciplines need to use constantly: the selection of information from source material and its reorganisation in another form, for example notes, tables, a diagram or a map. In some exercises the information required will be stated clearly. In other exercises the information will need to be inferred from clues in the text.

There are *composition* exercises in some units. These exercises provide practice in presenting information in straightforward written English. Such compositions should be planned by the student paragraph by paragraph. Model answers appear in the Teachers' Book.

There is a suggestion for *library work* at the end of each unit. These are tasks which require students to make use of reference books and to develop library skills.

TEACHERS' BOOK
Students who are learning English without a teacher can use the **English In Fact Teachers' Book** to assist them. The Teachers' Book contains suggestions for further study and a key to all the exercises.

M.A.L.

SUBMARINE PLUMBING

A straightforward new technique has been developed for laying pipelines in the North Sea. The method ensures that the ends of pipelines can be joined together accurately where previously they had been known to miss by as much as 100 metres.

5   As oil rigs have moved into deeper waters in recent years, connecting them to the coast has posed greater problems. The difficulty is laying the end of the pipe jutting out from the shore (the shore-pipe) to the spot where it meets the pipe from the rig. The meeting point is often 200 metres below the surface.

10   The pipeline is held by a strong cable from the pipe-laying ship, and it is gradually lowered to the sea-bed in a long curve. In shallow seas, engineers can calculate exactly where the pipe will come to rest on the sea-bed in relation to the point where they release it from the ship, but this method becomes inaccurate in deep waters. The two pipe sections

15 often miss each other so the whole operation has to start again. This can cost oil companies millions of pounds in lost time.

    The method designed to avoid these near misses is so simple that it seems strange nobody has thought of it before. The pipe-laying ship anchors near the spot where the two pipes have to be joined. It then

20 sets a course directly over this spot, dragging an anchored cable behind it. After a short distance on this course, the cable will have come to rest on top of the connection point. A diver fixes a marker on the cable to show where this happens. The ship then reverses, simultaneously reeling in the cable until the marker appears over the side of the ship.

25 At this point the ship stops, the end of the shore-pipe is fixed to the cable at the same place as the marker, and the ship returns along its original course, this time dragging the pipeline.

    Engineers can then be confident that it will meet the second pipe near enough the place intended.

1: Reference

What do the following words refer to?

    (a) they (line 3)
    (b) them (line 6)
    (c) it (line 8)
    (d) it (line 11)
    (e) they (line 13)
    (f) it (line 13)
    (g) This (line 15)
    (h) it (line 17)
    (i) it (line 18)
    (j) It (line 19)
    (k) it (line 21)
    (l) this (line 23)
    (m) it (line 28)

Pipe-laying barge Semac 1.

2: Vocabulary

Find words or phrases in the passage which could be replaced by the following without changing the meaning of the passage.

First paragraph:	(a) simple
	(b) method
	(c) before
Second paragraph:	(d) presented
	(e) projecting
Third paragraph:	(f) settle
Fourth paragraph:	(g) pulling
	(h) at the same time
	(i) winding
Fifth paragraph:	(j) feel sure

3: Transfer

(a) The diagrams A, B, C and D are arranged in the wrong order. Using the information in the passage, re-arrange them in the correct order:

ORDER	1	2	3	4
DIAGRAM				

(b) In each of the diagrams, show the movement of the ship forwards or backwards by drawing an arrow (→) pointing in the correct direction. If the ship is stationary in any diagram, put a cross. The arrows and crosses should be put in the box above the ship.

(c) In the circles in each diagram, label the shore-pipe with a letter S, the marker with a letter M, and the anchor with a letter A. Label all other items with a letter X.

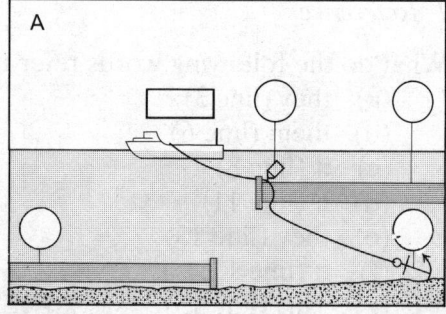

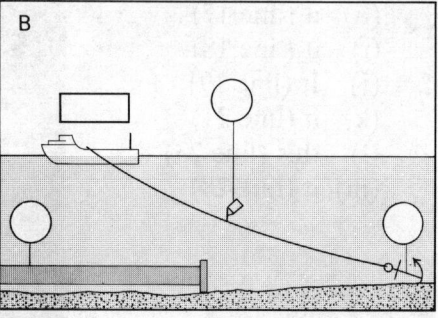

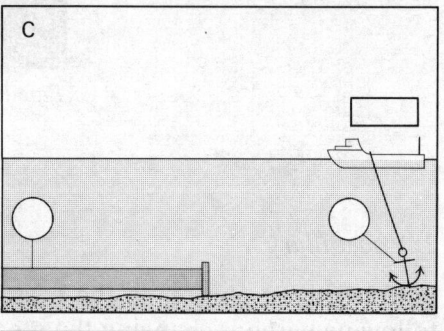

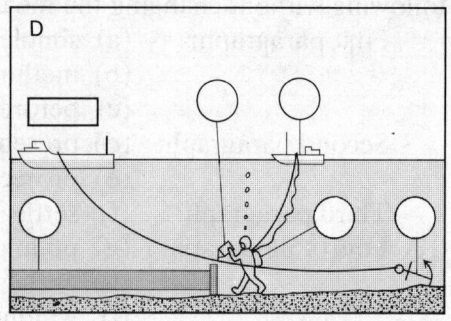

4: Composition

Write a set of instructions for the captain of a pipe-laying ship who is to carry out the operations described in the text and illustrated in the pictures. The first instruction is given you. Supply the rest.

1. Anchor the ship near the place where the two pipes will be joined.

2. _____

3. _____

4. _____

5. _____

6. _____

7. _____

8. _____

9. _____

10. _____

Library work

Find out (a) where the world's major oilfields are;
          (b) how petroleum originated in the earth's crust.

HUNTING METHODS OF THE BUSHMEN

The Bushmen are a people who inhabit a desert and semi-desert region of southern Africa. They are quite unlike the other peoples of this part of the world, for they are small, relatively light-skinned, and have protruding hindquarters.

5　　The Bushmen are nomadic, and maintain their existence by hunting. Their numbers have dwindled in the last few decades, but most of those who remain still lead the same way of life as their ancestors did millennia ago. They wander from place to place in small tribal groups, following and hunting the animals on which their existence depends.
10　Over the centuries they have devised many ingenious methods for hunting different kinds of animals.

Probably the most generally used of these methods is the hangman's noose snare. This is used for catching medium-sized animals such as leopards, zebras, and some species of antelope. A party of Bushmen
15　hunting for such animals lay a noose, or large ring of rope tied with a slip-knot, around a hole which they have dug in the ground near a clump of blue bushwood. After strewing sand and grass or leaves on the noose to hide it, they bend a stem of growing blue bushwood so that it forms a springy loop. The upper end of the stem, now almost
20　touching the ground, is tied to the base in such a way that the slightest touch on the rope will release the spring, pulling the end of the rope high into the air and tightening the noose around the body, neck or leg of the unfortunate animal.

The Bushmen have a completely different method for hunting
25　rhinoceros, for this animal is far too large and powerful to be trapped in this way: it would soon break out of the noose or uproot the stem of blue bushwood; and even if the rhinoceros could not climb out of the hole, the Bushmen would not be able to get close enough to kill it quickly and without risk of injury to themselves. Instead, when a
30　hunting party of Bushmen come across a solitary rhinoceros, they encourage it to give chase and then run backwards and forwards and in all directions, shouting and shrieking, to baffle and enrage it as much as possible. When the animal is totally bewildered, one of the hunters creeps stealthily up behind it and, with a swift, accurate slash with his
35　stone-age knife, cuts the tendons in its back legs. With these limbs

rendered useless, the rear part of the rhinoceros slumps to the ground under its own weight, and the Bushmen surround and finish off the helpless animal with their knives and spears.

1: Reference

What do the following words refer to?

(a) They (line 2)   (f) it (line 26)
(b) those (line 7)   (g) they (line 30)
(c) This (line 13)   (h) it (line 32)
(d) it (line 18)   (i) its own (line 37)
(e) it (line 19)

2: Vocabulary

Find words or phrases in the passage which could be replaced by the following without changing the meaning of the passage.

First paragraph: (a) live in
                          (b) completely distinct from
                          (c) projecting

Second paragraph: (d) keep alive
                          (e) fallen
                          (f) forefathers
                          (g) thousands of years
                          (h) clever

Third paragraph: (i) trap
                          (j) spreading
                          (k) curve

Fourth paragraph: (l) pull up
                          (m) single
                          (n) pursue them
                          (o) screaming
                          (p) confuse
                          (q) anger
                          (r) confused
                          (s) moves quietly
                          (t) blow
                          (u) made
                          (v) falls
                          (w) kill

3: Understanding

From the following sentences, select the true statements about the hunting of a rhinoceros, and then arrange them in the order in which the events they describe happen.

1. The animal is trapped in the hole.
2. The hunters chase the animal.
3. The hunters gather round the animal and kill it.
4. The animal becomes completely confused.
5. The animal breaks the noose.
6. The animal disturbs the rope.
7. The hunters make the animal angry and puzzled by running all over the place and making a lot of noise.
8. The hunters find a rhinoceros.
9. The animal pulls the blue bushwood stem out of the ground.
10. The animal's hind legs are cut so that they are no use to it.
11. The hunters let the animal chase them.
12. The spring is released.

4: Transfer

Study the pictures of the construction and operation of the hangman's noose snare. In one or more pictures the rope has been omitted, and in one or more pictures the blue bushwood stem utilised by the Bushmen has been omitted.

(a) Draw the rope and the blue bushwood stem in their correct positions in the pictures where they have been omitted.
(b) Arrange the pictures in their correct order.

ORDER	1	2	3	4
PICTURE				

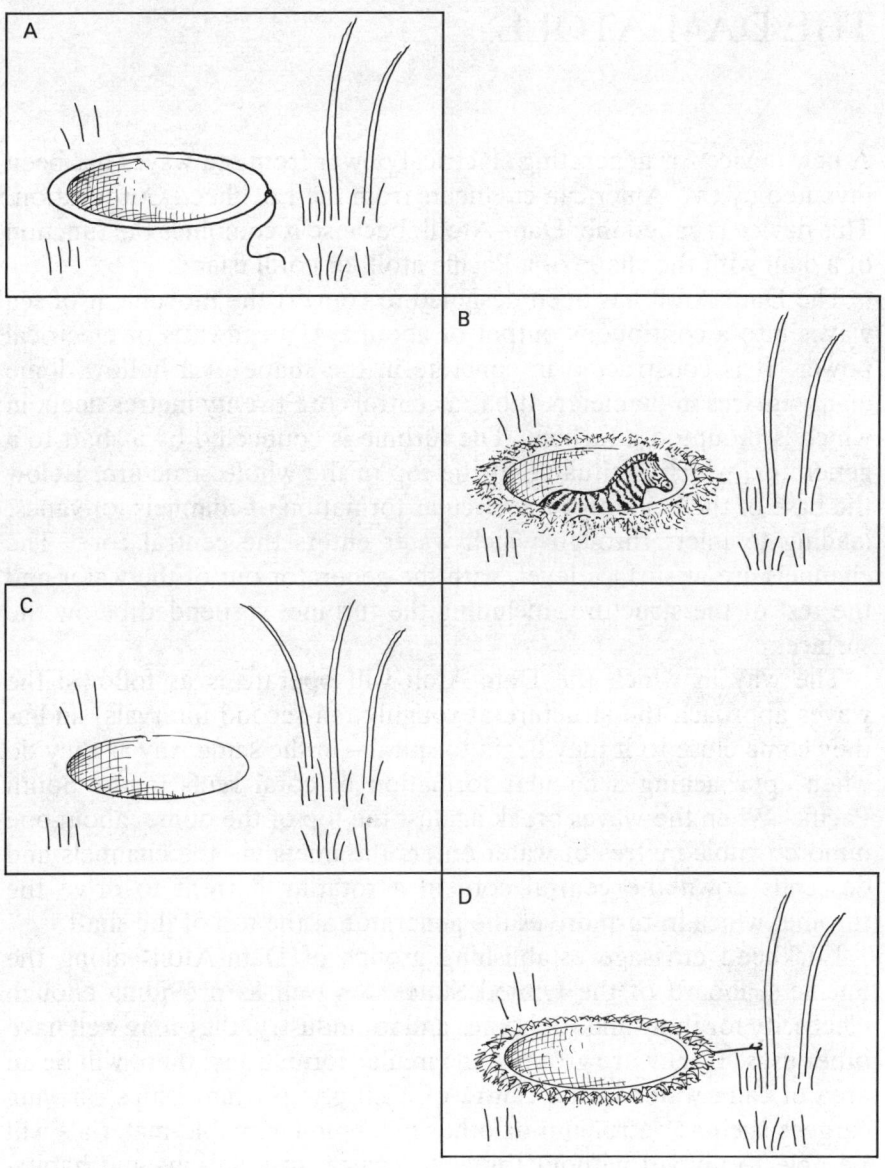

Library work

Find out (a) in which countries of southern Africa Bushmen may be
              found living today;

          (b) how the Bushman's protruding hindquarters are an asset
               to him.

THE DAM-ATOLL

A new device for generating electrical power from sea waves has been invented by two American engineers from the Lockheed Corporation. This device is called the 'Dam-Atoll', because it combines the function of a dam with the shape of a Pacific atoll, or coral island.

5   The Dam-Atoll has been designed to convert the movement of sea waves into a continuous output of about two megawatts of electrical power. It is constructed in concrete in the shape of a hollow dome eighty metres in diameter. It has a central core twenty metres deep, in which is mounted a turbine. The turbine is connected by a shaft to a

10   generator, which is situated at the top of the whole structure. Below the base of the generator is a circular formation of channels, or vanes, leading to inlets through which water enters the central core. The channels are at surface level, with the generator out of the water and the rest of the structure, including the turbine, suspended below the

15   surface.

The way in which the Dam-Atoll will operate is as follows: the waves approach the structure at roughly ten-second intervals, and as they come close to it they begin to spiral – in the same way as they do when approaching a circular formation of coral reefs in the South

20   Pacific. When the waves break against the top of the dome, about one hundred cubic metres of water enters the inlets via the channels and descends down the central core in a rotating current to drive the turbine, which in turn drives the generator at the top of the shaft.

Lockheed envisage establishing groups of Dam-Atolls along the

25   Pacific seaboard of the United States. As well as providing enough electricity for thousands of homes and for industry, they may well have other uses. If they are grouped in circular formations, there will be an area of calm water in the centre of each group where ships carrying cargoes such as petroleum or other highly inflammable materials will

30   be able to unload without threat to coastal installations and habitations. Also, if oil should be spilled by tankers or off-shore oil-rigs, the resulting oil-slicks would be drawn into the Dam-Atolls and held by them until the pollutant could be pumped out for disposal.

1:Vocabulary

Find words or phrases in the passage which could be replaced by the following without changing the meaning of the passage.

Second paragraph: (a) an upturned bowl

                              (b) hanging

Third paragraph: (c) move in ever-decreasing circles

Fourth paragraph: (d) look forward to

                              (e) coast

                              (f) danger

                              (g) buildings

                              (h) settlements

                              (i) structures for obtaining oil from beneath the sea-bed

                              (j) patches of floating oil

                              (k) It is possible to guess the meaning of the word 'atoll' from two phrases in the passage. The first phrase is in the first paragraph, and the second phrase is in the third paragraph. Write down these two phrases.

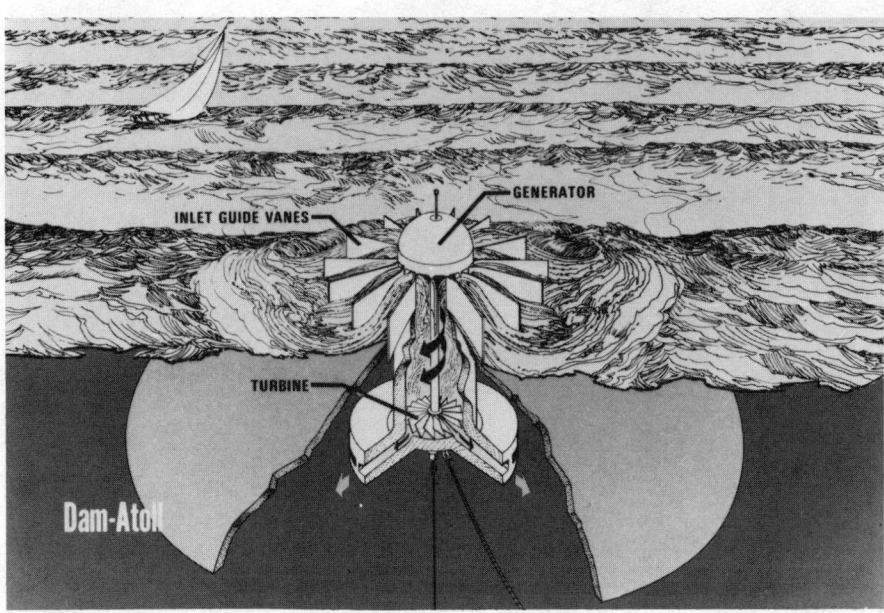

Diagram of a Dam-Atoll.

2: Transfer

Study the passage and the diagram of the vertical cross-section of a Dam-Atoll. Complete the key. Then, by means of three arrows, indicate the movement of water through the Dam-Atoll.

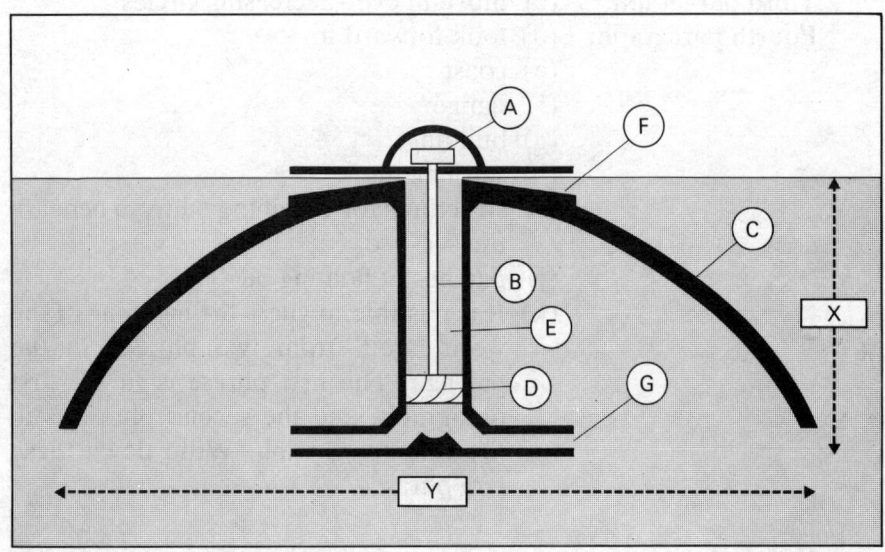

KEY

A _____

B _____

C _____

D _____

E _____

F _____

G _____

DIMENSIONS

X _____ metres

Y _____ metres

3: Understanding

Label the following statements true (T) or false (F) according to the passage.

_____ 1. The Dam-Atoll is an invention which will produce electricity from the movements of the surface of the sea.

_____ 2. The generator drives the turbine.

_____ 3. The Dam-Atoll rests on the sea-bed.

_____ 4. There are Dam-Atolls in the South Pacific.

_____ 5. The Dam-Atoll will be useful for removing oil pollution from the surface of the sea.

_____ 6. Circles of Dam-Atolls can provide sheltered waters for cargo ships.

_____ 7. Sea water enters the Dam-Atoll through the vanes and inlets.

_____ 8. Waves approach the Dam-Atoll in curved lines.

_____ 9. The water spins as it falls down the central core towards the generator.

_____ 10. Dam-Atolls are not yet in full production.

Library work

Find out (a) how a turbine works;

(b) about other schemes for obtaining power without using coal, oil, gas or nuclear energy.

SEA WATER CROPS

Scientists in California have been experimenting with growing barley on sand dunes, irrigated with sea water. Admittedly the yield was low – about 60% of the average for the world's barley crops – but it was a good deal better than nothing.

5   There is no biological incompatibility between land plants and sea water. Plenty of plants grow in estuaries and deltas, or in salty areas. So the scientists argued that it should be possible to produce barley that could tolerate, or even thrive on, sea water.

They started with a dramatic selection of the fittest plants. The basic
10 material was rather more than 4,000 seeds of a variety of barley called Composite XXI, which is the result of crossing 6,200 different varieties. The scientists argued that some of these seeds might tolerate sea water, so they grew the seeds in a large tank, adding salt water every three days after the first eight until such plants as were growing
15 at all were doing so in a solution of salt water three-quarters the strength of sea water.

There were few survivors: 94% of the plants did not produce seed. A similar experiment using a sea-water mix instead of salt killed off all but 10% of another batch of seeds.

20 But although few survived sea water, there were some which did. These were thinned by being grown in 85% sea water. Plants which emerged under these austere conditions were grown to seeding in a normal nutrient solution. Only 0.31% of the original seeds reached this stage.

25 These few survivors were sown in sand dunes, and watered with the Pacific Ocean. The ruthless selection had worked: every seed grew to a plant that looked normal, though a little stunted, and gave acceptable, if small, yields of grain.

As the scientists pointed out, there are strains of salt-resistant barley
30 scattered around the world, and a judicious selection from these could produce varieties with a better yield. The same process could be used to provide forage crops and, generally, to increase the botanical productivity of the world.

1: Reference

What do the following words and phrases refer to?
    (a) it (line 3)
    (b) it (line 7)
    (c) these seeds (line 12)
    (d) These (line 21)
    (e) these austere conditions (line 22)
    (f) these (line 30)

2: Vocabulary

Find words or phrases in the passage which could be replaced by the following without changing the meaning of the passage.

First paragraph:	(a)	hills
	(b)	product
	(c)	much
Second paragraph:	(d)	river mouths
	(e)	grow well in
Third paragraph:	(f)	be able to grow in
Fourth paragraph:	(g)	plants still living
	(h)	quantity
Fifth paragraph:	(i)	reduced to a smaller number
	(j)	survived
	(k)	difficult
	(l)	mixture of water and plant food
Sixth paragraph:	(m)	planted
	(n)	underdeveloped
Seventh paragraph:	(o)	careful choice
	(p)	crops for feeding farm animals

Barley.

3: Understanding

Select the twelve true statements about the barley-growing experiment from the sixteen statements below. Then arrange the true statements in the order in which the steps they describe occurred in the experiment.

1. Barley grows in salty conditions in different parts of the world.
2. Salt water was added on every third day.
3. 4,000 seeds of Composite XXXI were sown.
4. The parallel experiment using sea water was more successful by 4%.
5. The amount of sea water was increased by 10%.
6. Forage crops were produced.
7. Composite XXI was produced from the cross-fertilisation of 6,200 different varieties of barley.
8. The seeding plants were only 94% after sea water had been added.
9. The seeds of the successful plants were grown in a non-salty solution.
10. The plants were shorter than normal, but they produced a reasonable quantity of seed.
11. The seeds were planted in a tank.
12. Of the original quantity of seeds, only one in 300 survived.
13. The solution of 75% salt water reduced the plants producing seed to 6%.
14. They were watered with sea water.
15. The seeds were left for eight days.
16. The seeds were planted in the sand hills beside the sea.

4: Summary

What was the purpose of the scientists' experiment? Answer in 25 to 30 words.

Library work

Find out (a) what kind of plant barley is;
         (b) in what parts of the world it is grown;
         (c) what it is used for.

HAILSTORMS OVER KENYA

Some scientists have been trying to find out what makes hailstorms so frequent in the tea-growing districts of Kenya. The tea plantations of the Nandi Hills and around Kericho in western Kenya have an average of 132 days of hailstorms per year, which is far higher than anywhere
5   else in the world.

These hailstorms cause immense damage to the tea plantations, for the hailstones batter the tender shoots of the bushes so violently that they are broken off, and the best source of high quality tea is lost.

The scientists are working on the theory that, as the tea-pickers walk
10   between the rows of bushes picking the leaves, with their feet they disturb the dry particles of leaf that are lying on the ground. These dry particles, which are little more than organic dust, rise into the air and are drawn up by a rising airstream into the thunderclouds that are frequently overhead in equatorial regions such as Kenya. There these
15   particles form nuclei on which droplets of water are able to form. But why should these droplets freeze and turn into hailstones, and not simply fall as rain, which would not be so destructive? The explanation seems to involve two factors.

The first of these is altitude. Most of Kenya is a plateau, and the
20   area where most of the tea plantations are located is over 2,000 metres above sea level. From this altitude, the droplets do not have to rise very far before they enter a layer of the atmosphere where the temperature is below zero. The other factor is the nature of the particle of tea-leaf, and in particular its effectiveness as a nucleus in
25   the formation of a water droplet.

The scientists have been experimenting with different kinds of particles in a test chamber of moist air. These include, as well as the leaf dust from various trees, crystals of silver iodide, which for some time have been sprayed from aircraft into clouds to cause the
30   formation of water droplets that will fall as rain. For water droplets to form on silver iodide crystals, the air temperature must be as low as between $-8°$ and $-10°C$. Organic particles from the indigenous forests of Kenya require a temperature of $-8°C$, and so are much more effective than the leaf dust from eucalyptus trees, which can function
35   as nuclei only below $-11°C$. Best of all, however, is tea-leaf dust,

which requires a temperature of only −5°C.

Two benefits may spring from this scientific work. The first is that some way may be found to prevent the tea-leaf dust from rising into the air above the Kenyan tea plantations so that the incidence of hailstorms can be considerably reduced. And the second is that, if some efficient way for collecting the tea-leaf dust can be devised, the tea-leaf dust can be used for seeding clouds – that is, sprayed from aircraft to stimulate rainfall on to drought-stricken farmland.

1: Reference

What do the following words refer to?
- (a) they (line 8)
- (b) they (line 10)
- (c) these (line 19)
- (d) they (line 22)
- (e) its (line 24)
- (f) These (line 27)
- (g) The first (line 37)

2: Vocabulary

Find words or phrases in the passage which could be replaced by the following without changing the meaning of the passage.

Second paragraph:	(a) severe
	(b) strike
Third paragraph:	(c) lands around the Equator
Fourth paragraph:	(d) height above sea level
	(e) a high, flat region
Fifth paragraph:	(f) testing
	(g) native
Sixth paragraph:	(h) frequency
	(i) worked out
	(j) cause
	(k) dried up

Tea-picking in Kenya.

3: Transfer

Fill in the table below to show the temperatures at which the different kinds of particles mentioned in the passage begin to function as nuclei for water droplets. Arrange the entries according to temperature.

Type of Particle	Temperature of Droplet Formation

4: Transfer

Complete the diagram below so that it illustrates the seeding of clouds to produce rainfall.

Library work

Find out (a) which are the major tea-growing areas of the world;

(b) which three countries are the leading consumers of tea per head of the population.

PETROL TANKS

The average motorist has no conception of the construction of his car's petrol tank. He does not know what shape it is or what is inside it, and has only a vague idea of where it is. The only part of it that he sees regularly is the top end of the filler pipe when he stops to buy petrol.

5   The petrol tank fitted in most cars is made of two pieces of mild sheet steel. The steel is coated on both sides with lead or tin to prevent corrosion. The two pieces are cut out and pressed into shape with regular ribs and hollows to give them rigidity. On to the bottom section baffles are welded. These are a system of steel walls or barriers
10   which prevent the petrol being thrown violently from one end of the tank to the other as the car turns a sharp corner or comes to a sudden halt.

Two methods are employed for joining the top and bottom sections of the tank together. The first is by rolling or riveting the flattened
15   edges, or seams, and then soldering the joined seams to seal them. The alternative is by welding the seams. After attaching the filler pipe and then inserting the petrol gauge into a hole in the top, the tank is fitted to the body of the car, usually by means of a pair of steel belts.

Recently some German motor manufacturers have been fitting their
20   cars with plastic petrol tanks. The type of plastic used is high-density polyethylene. Moulds are specially made for each model of car on the production line, and the liquid polyethylene is blown into the mould and allowed to set. This is a single operation, whereas the putting together of a steel tank consists, as we have seen, of several opera-
25   tions. Thus the production of plastic petrol tanks is both quicker and cheaper than that of steel ones.

But plastic tanks have several other advantages over steel tanks. Plastic can be moulded into complex shapes so that every available cubic centimetre of the petrol tank compartment is utilised. A car
30   fitted with a plastic tank has less weight to carry than one fitted with a steel tank.

It has commonly been thought that a plastic tank is more dangerous in a fire than a steel tank. In fact, the reverse is probably true, because, whereas the latter will resist the flames until the pressure inside is so

35   great that there is an explosion, the plastic tank will melt and release the petrol and its vapour in a more even flow and with less catastrophic results.

1: Reference

What do the following words refer to?
- (a) it (lines 2 and 3)
- (b) them (line 8)
- (c) These (line 9)
- (d) The first (line 14)
- (e) them (line 15)
- (f) This (line 23)
- (g) one (line 30)
- (h) the reverse (line 33)
- (i) the latter (line 34)

2: Vocabulary

Find words or phrases in the passage which could be replaced by the following without changing the meaning of the passage.

First paragraph:	(a) idea
	(b) rough
Second paragraph:	(c) covered
	(d) stiffness
	(e) stop
Fourth paragraph:	(f) become hard
	(g) is made up of
Fifth paragraph:	(h) made use of
Sixth paragraph:	(i) damaging

3: Technical vocabulary

Below are some definitions and diagrams. These explain or illustrate the meanings of some technical words in the passage. The words themselves are listed at the end of the question. Write the correct words in the spaces provided.

(a)

(b)

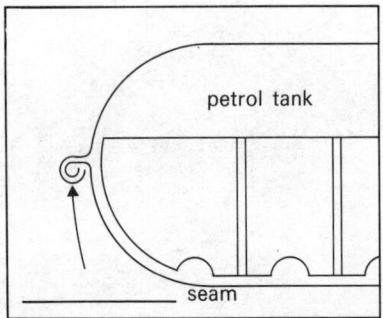
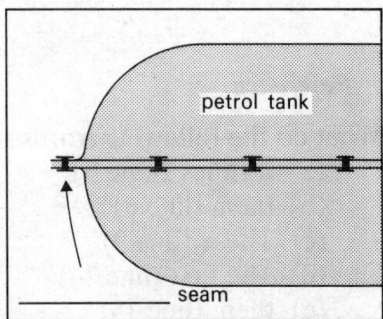

(c) _____is a method of joining pieces of hard metal or filling holes in harder metal by means of melting and applying a soft alloy containing lead.

(d) _____are hollow forms into which materials in a liquid state are poured to solidify into required shapes.

(e) _____is a method of joining pieces of metal by means of heat.

(f) _____is the process of the wearing away of a material by chemical action.

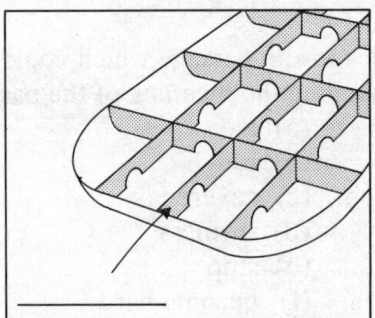

(*Technical words*: welding; baffles; rolled; moulds; riveted; soldering; corrosion.)

4: Understanding

Select from the following statements the nine true ones about the making of a steel petrol tank, and then arrange them in the correct sequence.
1. The filler pipe is attached.
2. The seams of the two sections are riveted to prevent leaks.
3. The steel is cut into two sheets.
4. The seams of the two sections are rolled.
5. Liquid polyethylene is poured into a mould.
6. The seams of the two sections are welded and soldered.
7. The petrol gauge is fitted into the top of the tank.
8. The two sheets are stamped into shape.
9. The rolled seams are soldered to prevent leaks.
10. The polyethylene tank is taken out of the mould.
11. The seams of the two sections are rolled and riveted.
12. The polyethylene sets in the mould.
13. The baffles are welded in position.
14. Both sides of the sheet are coated with a non-corrosive metal.
15. The baffles are fitted together and placed in the bottom section.

5: Transfer

Complete the following table by putting ticks in the appropriate places.

Qualities	Steel tanks	Polyethylene tanks
1. Quicker to make		
2. Cheaper to make		
3. Stronger	✓	
4. More easily shaped		
5. Lighter		
6. More resistant to fire		
7. Less likely to explode		

(One tick has been put in as an example.)

RAISING A TEMPLE

In July 1977, Lieutenant-Commander David Bartlett was ordered to
lead a diving team from the British navy to co-operate with the
Egyptian navy in rescuing the 2,000-year-old Temple of Augustus
Caesar from the waters of Aswan.

5   The temple, situated on what was once the island of Philae in the
River Nile at Aswan, had been under water since the building of the
Low Aswan Dam in 1902. With the completion of the High Dam in
1970, the island was almost completely submerged.

The intention was to raise the temple and reconstruct it on a nearby
10   island. However, this looked almost impossible. First, where was the
temple? All that was visible was a flat surface of water, and six metres
below that was a flat surface of mud.

Research turned up some photographs taken by a British archaeological expedition in 1901. A distinctively shaped rock, clearly visible in
15   one of the photographs, was still above the water-line. Using this,
Bartlett could judge the likely site of the temple. The area was marked
out with buoys and posts. Then they felt for building remains beneath
the bed of the reservoir with iron probes. Soon, what had felt like soft
mud felt like concrete.

20   Before the temple blocks could be located, marked, attached by
cables to airbags, and lifted to the surface, the mud had to be
penetrated. By the second week in October, work had started. The
divers worked in pairs, one blasting the mud with a water jet, and the
other removing the loosened mud with an airlift – a sort of underwater
25   vacuum cleaner. But this disturbance of the mud layer created a
perpetual state of zero visibility, so that the divers had to work solely
by touch.

On the hundredth day, the first of the blocks was raised to the
surface. When the whole operation was completed, 2,000 tonnes of
30   mud had been pumped from the site, and all 320 blocks of stone had
been raised from beneath the waters of Aswan.

Recovery of a block from the Temple of Augustus Caesar.

1: Understanding

Select the true sentences and arrange them in the order in which the events they describe happened.

1. The divers started work late in October 1977.
2. The Aswan High Dam was built to replace the Aswan Low Dam.
3. The temple was situated on the highest part of the island of Philae.
4. Part of the temple was still above the water when Bartlett arrived at Aswan.
5. The Aswan Low Dam was built in the early years of the twentieth century.
6. The temple was built towards the end of the first century B.C.
7. A group of British archaeologists took photographs of the temple at the beginning of the twentieth century.
8. The task of raising the temple took a hundred days.
9. Bartlett studied the old photographs and the site itself, and worked out approximately where the temple was.
10. Lieutenant-Commander Bartlett was chosen to lead a group of British navy divers.
11. The temple was completely submerged by the waters above the Aswan Low Dam.
12. The temple ruins were buried under water and mud.
13. Philae was completely submerged by the waters behind the Aswan High Dam.
14. The Aswan High Dam was built about seventy years after the Low Dam was built.
15. An archaeological expedition visited Aswan on the completion of the Low Dam.

2: Transfer

Study the diagram, and look again at the passage. Shown on the diagram are seven possible water-levels in relation to the island of Philae. These are A, B, C, D, E, F, and G. Decide which of these were the likely water-levels in 1895, 1935, and 1975.

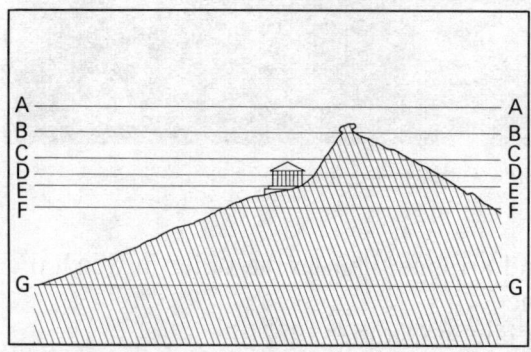

Water-level in 1895: _____
Water-level in 1935: _____
Water-level in 1975: _____

Then mark with a broken line (– – – –) the probable level of mud in 1975.

3: Composition

Column A is a list of objects, such as pieces of equipment used by the diving team. Column B is a list of actions or processes in the raising of the temple. Using *all* the words in these columns, write an account of how the divers carried out this operation. (Some words may be used more than once; and you may have to change the form of some of the words; for example, putting the verb in the correct tense, or making a noun plural.)

A	B
block of stone	mark out
post	suck up
cable	fasten
airbag	feel for
ruins	find
airlift	blast
buoy	mark
water jet	get through
mud	raise
iron probe	

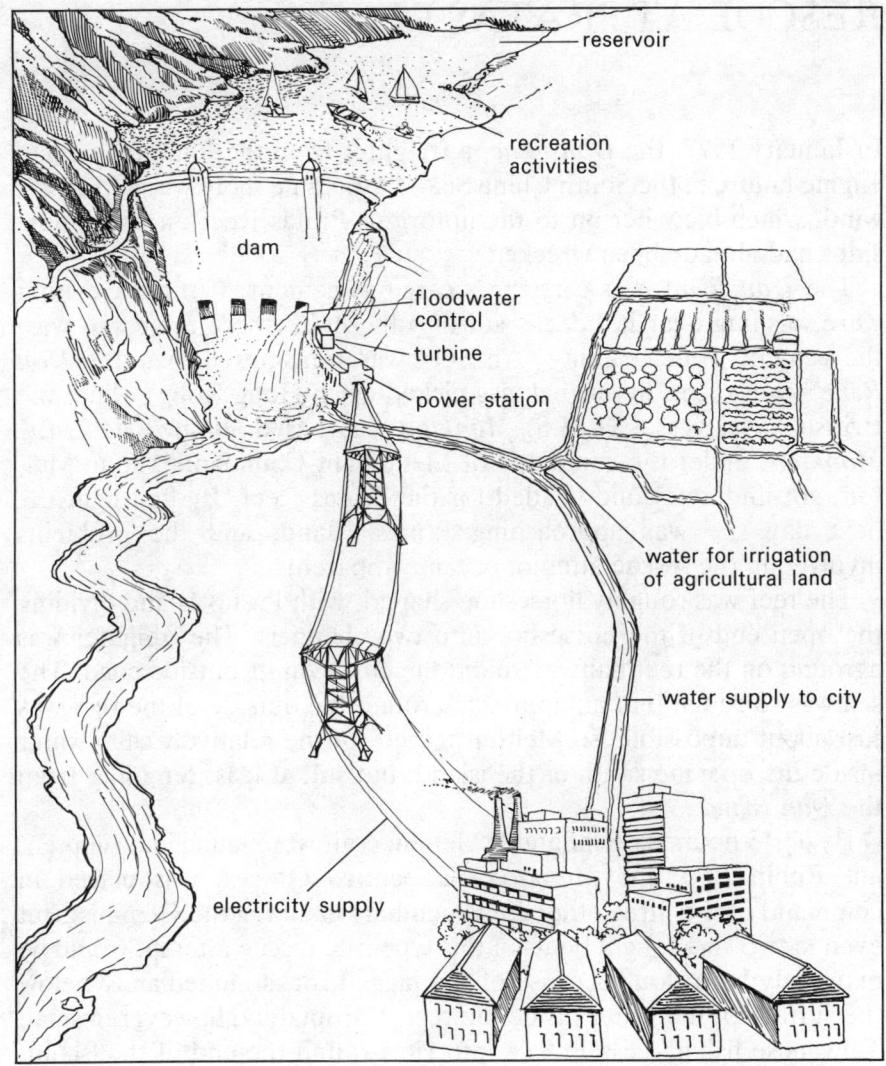

Labels in diagram:
- reservoir
- recreation activities
- dam
- floodwater control
- turbine
- power station
- water for irrigation of agricultural land
- water supply to city
- electricity supply

Library work

Find out (a) about the course and size of the River Nile;
         (b) why the Aswan High Dam was built;
         (c) about the dependence of Egypt on the River Nile.

Using the information contained in the diagram and any other information from the library, write an account of the different ways in which the building of dams is beneficial to man.

RESCUE AT PRATAS REEF

In January 1977, the *Don Rene*, a freighter from the Philippines, had engine failure in the South China Sea. At the time there was a force-six wind, which blew her on to the notorious Pratas Reef on which nine ships had already been wrecked.

5 The *Don Rene* was carrying a cargo of cement. If the waves that were washing over her decks got into the hold where the cargo was, the cement would solidify. An SOS was transmitted over the *Don Rene*'s radio, and this signal was picked up in Hong Kong, where the British naval vessel H.M.S. *Monkton* was based. Immediately, the

10 *Monkton*, under the command of Lieutenant-Commander John Melton, got underway and headed for the Pratas Reef. By first light the next day she was approaching Pratas Island, and the problems involved in the rescue attempt became apparent.

The reef was roughly horseshoe-shaped, with Pratas Island dividing

15 the open end of the horseshoe into two channels. The freighter was aground on the reef halfway round the curve on its outside edge. The sea was so rough that an approach around the outside of the reef was just about impossible, so Melton steered for the relatively calm water inside the opening south of the island, but still at least ten miles from

20 the *Don Rene*.

By 07.15 hours, two inflatable Gemini craft were launched. Lieutenant Robin Ball, the *Monkton's* Executive Officer, was placed in command of the three other crew members manning the Geminis. But even in two small, light boats of this type, the rescue attempt would be

25 extremely hazardous because of the jagged rocks immediately below the surface of the water inside the reef. Fortunately, however, a small Taiwanese fishing vessel came into view round the end of the island, and Melton was able to call on it for assistance. But even with the help of the trawler, whose captain knew the reef like the back of his hand, it

30 took the rescue team six hours to find a passage through the shoals and to come within a mile of the freighter. Now, at the inside edge of the reef, a further difficulty presented itself.

It was just after low water, and there was not enough clearance over the shelf of rock for the Geminis to avoid having their bottoms ripped

35 open. For the last mile to the *Don Rene*, Lieutenant Ball and his team

had to disembark and scramble over the coral reef, dragging the Geminis after them.

By the time the crew of the wrecked freighter had been ferried back to safety, the whole rescue operation had taken the best part of a day.

1: Reference

What do the following words refer to?
- (a) her (line 3)
- (b) she (line 12)
- (c) this type (line 24)
- (d) it (line 28)
- (e) it (line 29)
- (f) them (line 37)

2: Vocabulary

Below are the definitions of some words in the passage. These words are listed at the end of the question. Write the correct words in the spaces provided.
- (a) _____ is the process of getting off a ship or boat.
- (b) A _____ is a shallow place in the sea, especially where there is sand or rock just below the surface of the water.
- (c) An _____ is a signal asking for help, usually sent by means of a radio transmitter.
- (d) A _____ is the goods carried by a ship.
- (e) A _____ is a type of ship used for fishing by pulling nets behind it.
- (f) A _____ is a line of rocks or coral just above or just below the surface of the sea.
- (g) A _____ is a ship which has as its main function the transportation of goods.
- (h) _____ is a hard pink, red or white substance composed of the remains of dead sea creatures called polyps. It is to be found in shallow tropical waters.

(*Words*: coral; disembarkation; SOS; shoal; cargo; trawler; reef; freighter).

H.M.S. Monkton.

3: Understanding

Of the following sixteen sentences, twelve are true according to the passage. Say which are the four false sentences. Then arrange the true sentences in the order in which the events they describe happened.

1. A fishing boat was sailing nearby.
2. The *Don Rene* was driven on to a reef by a strong wind.
3. The crew of the *Don Rene* were taken aboard the *Monkton*.
4. The *Monkton* left Hong Kong.
5. The *Don Rene* was carrying cement.
6. Two small boats left the *Monkton*.
7. The engines of the *Don Rene* broke down.
8. The fishing boat led the two rescue boats through the shallow waters.
9. The water was rough inside the reef.
10. The fishing boat went on the Pratas Reef.
11. The fishing boat captain agreed to help in the rescue of the crew of the freighter.
12. Nine ships had already been abandoned on the reef.
13. The British sailors got out of their boats and walked across the reef.
14. The *Monkton* arrived near the reef before sunrise.
15. Lieutenant Ball was the commander of the *Monkton*.
16. The *Monkton* went aground on the Pratas Reef.

4: Transfer

On the map mark the positions of the *Monkton* and the *Don Rene* and the route of the rescue team from the *Monkton* to the *Don Rene*. Use the symbols in the key to do this. One of the symbols in the key is not labelled; complete the key with a suitable word or phrase.

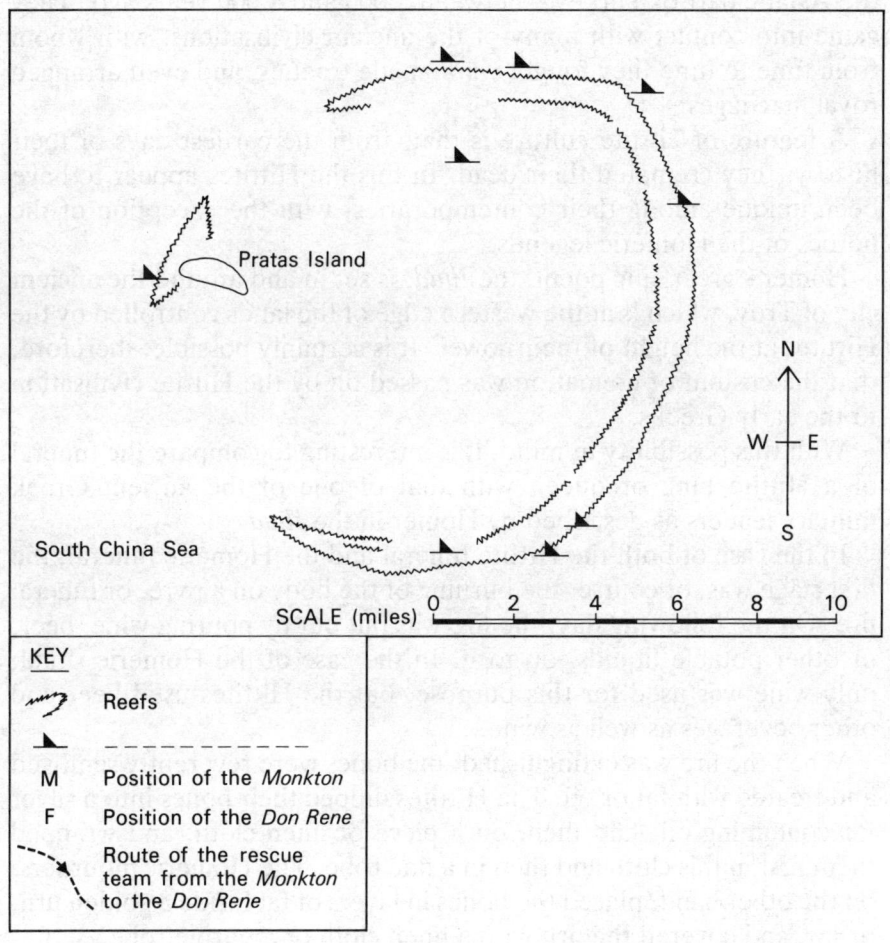

Library work

Find out how an atoll is formed.

HITTITE AND HOMERIC FUNERALS

The Hittites were a people who lived in central Anatolia – what is now
the Asiatic part of Turkey – between 3,000 and 4,000 years ago. They
came into contact with many of the ancient civilisations, with whom
from time to time they fought wars, made treaties, and even arranged
5   royal marriages.

A feature of Hittite culture is that, from the earliest days of their
history, they cremated their dead. In this the Hittites appear to have
been unique among their contemporaries, with the exception of the
heroes of the Homeric legends.

10   Homer's great epic poem, the *Iliad*, is set in and around the ancient
city of Troy, which is at the western edge of the lands controlled by the
Hittites at the height of their power. It is certainly possible, therefore,
that the custom of cremation was passed on by the Hittite civilisation
to the early Greeks.

15   With this possibility in mind, it is interesting to compare the funeral
of a Hittite king or queen with that of one of the ancient Greek
military leaders as described by Homer in the *Iliad*.

In the case of both the Hittite funeral and the Homeric funeral, the
first stage was, of course, the burning of the body on a pyre, or funeral
20   fire. On the following day, the fire was put out by pouring wine, beer,
or other potable liquids, on to it. In the case of the Homeric ritual,
only wine was used for this purpose, but the Hittites used beer and
other beverages as well as wine.

When the fire was extinguished, the bones were reverently removed
25   and treated with fat or oil. The Hittites dipped their bones into a silver
jar containing oil, laid them on a piece of linen cloth, and wrapped
them first in this cloth and then in a fine robe. The Homeric mourners,
on the other hand, placed the bones in layers of fat inside a golden urn,
or jar, and covered the urn with a linen cloth or a purple robe.

30   The next stage was to place the wrapped remains in a burial
chamber. In the Hittite burial chamber the bundle of bones was placed
on a chair or a stool, the former if it was a man's bones, and the latter
if it was a woman's. But the Homeric urn was simply placed on the
floor of the chamber and covered with the ceremonial cloth. In both

35 cases, the burial chamber was built of stone, but the Hittites, unlike the Homeric mourners, did not make a barrow over the chamber.

After the remains of the dead person had been placed in the chamber, both the Hittite and the Homeric funeral ended with a feast, but these feasts, apart from the eating and drinking, were of a different
40 character. Whereas the Hittites conducted a series of religious rites including the sacrifice of animals to the Sun-goddess, the friends and relatives of the dead Homeric hero took part in athletic competitions.

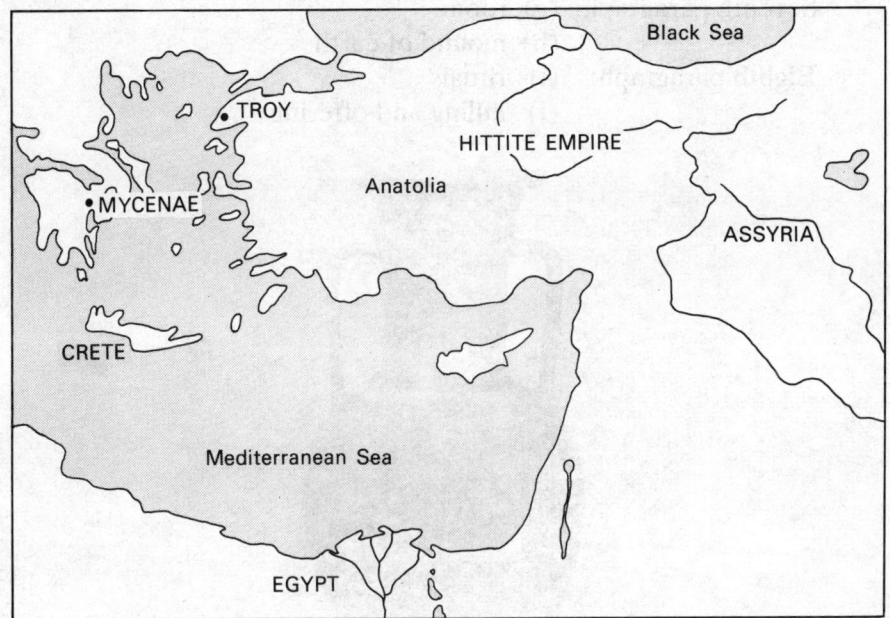

1: Reference

What do the following words refer to?

    (a) they (line 4)
    (b) this (line 7)
    (c) their (line 12)
    (d) that (line 16)
    (e) it (line 21)
    (f) them (line 26)
    (g) the latter (line 32)

2: Vocabulary

Find words or phrases in the passage that could be replaced by the
following without changing the meaning of the passage.

Second paragraph: (a) burned
                      (b) alone
                      (c) other peoples of their time

Fifth paragraph: (d) beverages

Sixth paragraph: (e) friends and relatives of the dead person
                      (f) pot (two possibilities)

Seventh paragraph: (g) room
                      (h) mound of earth

Eighth paragraph: (i) rituals
                      (j) killing and offering

Athenian geometric amphora, eighth century B.C.

3: Transfer

The following is a list of stages of Hittite and Homeric funerals.
Decide which are Hittite and which are Homeric. Then, in the correct
place in the table below, write the letter for each stage. Stages 1, 3 and
7, which are the same in both funerals, are already written in.

A. The bones are dipped in oil.
B. The bones are placed on a chair or stool.
C. The fire is extinguished with wine.
D. The bones are put in a golden urn.
E. The bones are wrapped in fat.
F. The burial chamber is covered with earth.
G. The mourners feast and make offerings to the gods.
H. The bones are wrapped in a garment.
I. The mourners feast and compete in sports.
J. The bones are wrapped in linen.
K. The urn is covered loosely with a cloth.
L. The fire is extinguished with various potable liquids.

STAGE	HITTITE FUNERAL	HOMERIC FUNERAL
1	The body is burnt	The body is burnt
2		
3	The bones are taken from the pyre	The bones are taken from the pyre
4		
5		
6		
7	The bones are put in the burial chamber	The bones are put in the burial chamber
8		
9		

Library work

Find out (a) how and when the capital city of the Hittite Empire was discovered in the nineteenth century;
   (b) who Homer was and when he lived;
   (c) if there is a basis of fact to the stories contained in Homer's epic poems.

LOCUSTS

Locusts are medium-sized to large insects belonging to the order *Orthoptera*, which includes the grasshoppers and crickets. Insects of this order have powerful jaws and, usually, hind legs well developed for jumping.

5　　There is no significant structural difference between the body of a locust and that of a grasshopper. The crucial difference is in behaviour. Grasshoppers maintain the same regular way of life generation after generation; but locusts, after several generations of a placid, solitary existence, suddenly swarm and migrate, devastating the

10　vegetation in their path.

Locusts inhabit the warmer parts of the world. The three most studied species are the desert locust (*Schistocerca gregaria*), the migratory locust (*Locusta migratoria*), and the red locust (*Nomadacris septemfasciata*). The desert locust occurs in northern Africa, the

15　Arabian Peninsula, and eastwards as far as India. The migratory locust has an even wider distribution: it lives in a huge area of the world including southern Europe, West Africa, southern U.S.S.R., China, Japan, the Philippines, and Australia. The red locust, however, is confined to central and southern Africa.

20　These three species of locusts have two phases, in which not only their behaviour differs, but their physical appearance does as well. The two phases are the solitarious phase, when the locusts live quietly and as individuals in one location in the manner of ordinary grasshoppers, and the gregarious phase, when the locusts gather together in vast

25　swarms and migrate to new territory which may be hundreds of kilometres away.

In general, a solitarious locust has a uniform colouring, usually green or light brown. A gregarious locust, however, has bold, black markings, on a background of yellow in the case of the desert locust

30　and the red locust, or orange in the case of the migratory locust. The migratory locust and the desert locust have a high crest on the pronotum in their solitarious phase, whereas in their gregarious phase the pronotum is saddle-shaped like that of the red locust and has no crest. The locusts also differ in size in their two phases. The desert

35　locust, the red locust and the female migratory locust are larger in

their solitarious phase than in their gregarious phase, but with the male migratory locust the reverse is the case. A general characteristic of the gregarious phase is that the hind femur, the powerful leg component specially adapted for jumping, is smaller than it is in the
40   solitarious phase, when it projects beyond the end of the abdomen.

1: Reference

What do the following words refer to?
    (a) that (line 6)
    (b) it (line 16)
    (c) their (line 21)
    (d) their (line 32)
    (e) their (line 36)
    (f) it (line 39)

2: Vocabulary

Find words or phrases in the passage which could be replaced by the following without a noticeable change of meaning.

First paragraph:	(a) rear
Second paragraph:	(b) important
	(c) vital
	(d) follow
	(e) quiet
	(f) crowd together
	(g) destroying
Third paragraph:	(h) limited
Fourth paragraph:	(i) travel
Fifth paragraph:	(j) plain

3: Transfer

On the map below, the distribution of two species of locusts is shown by two kinds of shading. Draw the appropriate kind of shading beside each name in the key.

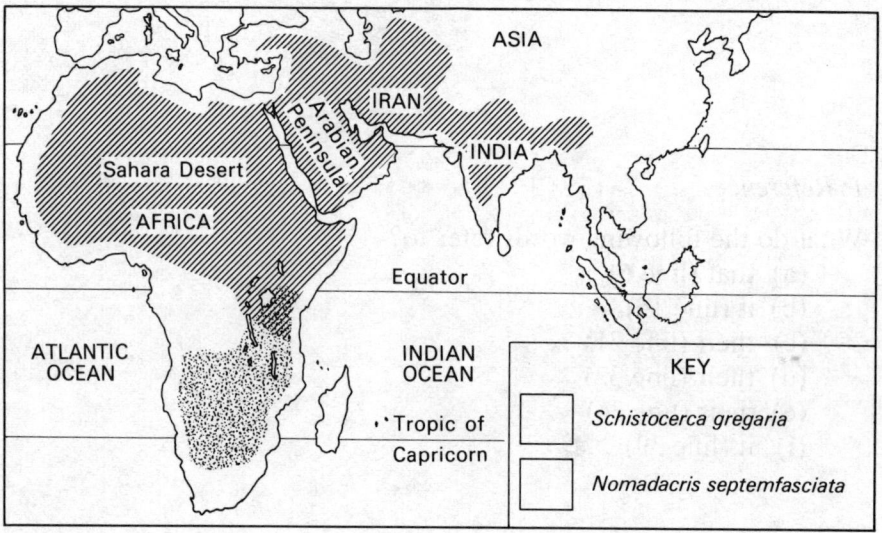

KEY

Schistocerca gregaria

Nomadacris septemfasciata

4: Transfer

Here are drawings of the female *Locusta migratoria*, one showing it in its gregarious phase, and the other showing it in its solitarious phase. Identify the two phases by writing the appropriate word in the space under each diagram. Then label the parts of the locust according to the key, using the letters A, C, F and P. Write X for any part not given in the key. Fill all the circles.

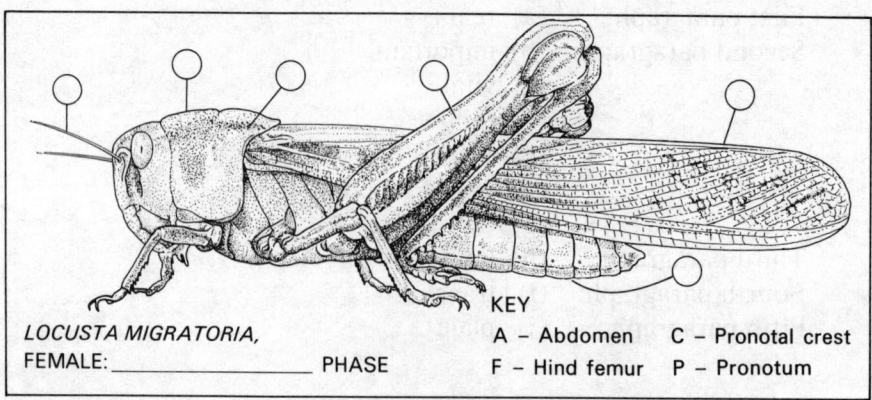

LOCUSTA MIGRATORIA, FEMALE: _____ PHASE

KEY

A – Abdomen   C – Pronotal crest

F – Hind femur   P – Pronotum

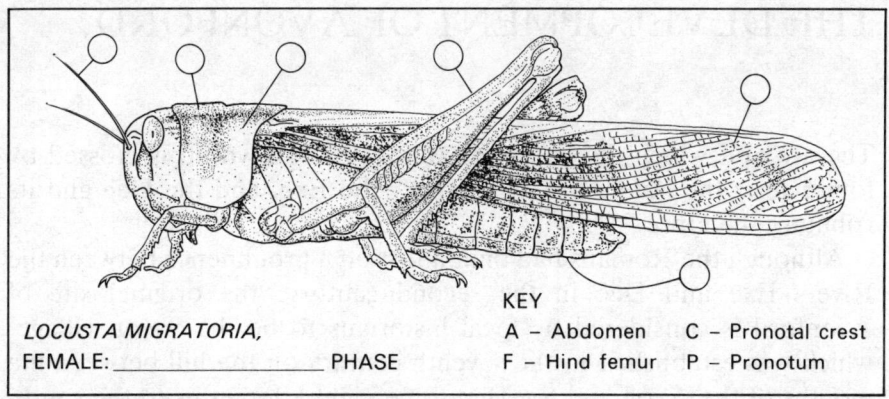

LOCUSTA MIGRATORIA,
FEMALE: _____ PHASE

KEY

A – Abdomen   C – Pronotal crest
F – Hind femur   P – Pronotum

5: Transfer

Complete the following table. Write the names of the three species of locust at the head of the columns on the right, and write the following terms in their correct places in the body of the table:

   Black and orange; black and yellow; crested; larger; saddle-shaped; smaller; uniform.

CHARACTERISTICS				
COLOUR	GREG			
	SOL			
SIZE	GREG			
	SOL			
PRONOTUM	GREG			
	SOL			
HIND FEMUR	GREG			
	SOL			

Library work

Find out about methods of controlling locusts.

THE DEVELOPMENT OF AVONFORD

The area on which the city of Avonford has grown up is crossed by four rivers, the Avon and its tributary the Exe, and the Dee and its tributary the Ouse.

Although the Romans had built a fort on a prominence between the
5   Rivers Exe and Dee in the second century, the original site of Avonford is considered by local historians to be the Saxon village, which was established in the seventh century on the hill between the mouths of the Avon and the Dee some eight kilometres to the south. There may have been an early British settlement on the high ground to
10   the west across the mouth of the Avon, but this was probably abandoned when the Romans left Britain early in the fifth century.

The Normans came to Britain in the middle of the eleventh century, and in order to control the Saxon population of the area they built a castle at the western end of the long, curved hill on the eastern bank of
15   the Dee – in fact, just across the river from the site of the Roman fort.

In the fourteenth century, a wooden bridge was built across the Dee immediately below the place where it is joined by the Ouse; and about a hundred years later Dog Island was connected by stone bridges to both banks of the Avon. Thus communications between Avonford and
20   the regions to the east and west were greatly improved, especially after the replacement of the wooden Dee bridge by a stone one about a kilometre further south at the beginning of the sixteenth century. These improvements in communications led to the northward expansion of the town on to the area between the two river systems known as
25   Flatfields.

In the early part of the eighteenth century, a harbour was developed in the sheltered waters between the eastern shore of the mouth of the Dee and Green Island, and in the next fifty years the town spread into the area east of the mouth of the Dee, Deeside.
30   In 1830, iron ore was discovered in the hills north-west of Avonford, to the west of the River Avon, and this triggered the growth of industry on the plain at the foot of the southern slopes of those hills. This industrial development in Brownvale greatly increased the contribution of Avonford to the British economy, and this was recognised
35   early in the twentieth century when Avonford was raised to the status

of City. Since that auspicious occasion, it has expanded to include Deeside, Dog Island, Brownvale, and Castletown, the district north of the hill between the Dee and the Ouse. Because the old harbour in the Green Island channel was inadequate for the commercial needs of a
40 twentieth century city, a new harbour, called Newport, has been constructed in the bay immediately to the west of the mouth of the Avon.

1: Vocabulary

Deduce from the text and the map the correct explanation of the following words.

1. tributary (lines 2 and 3): (a) a larger river flowing into a smaller one;
  (b) a smaller river flowing into a larger one;
  (c) the joining of two rivers.

2. prominence (line 4): (a) a piece of land higher than the surrounding land;
  (b) a river valley;
  (c) a piece of land lower than the surrounding land.

3. settlement (line 9): (a) a village;
  (b) a deserted area;
  (c) a piece of high ground.

4. abandoned (line 11): (a) occupied;
  (b) left;
  (c) developed.

5. expansion (line 23): (a) reduction;
  (b) occupation;
  (c) growth.

6. triggered (line 31): (a) started;
  (b) slowed down;
  (c) developed.

7. auspicious (line 36): (a) doubtful;
  (b) ordinary;
  (c) celebrated.

8. inadequate (line 39): (a) unbeneficial;
  (b) insufficient;
  (c) sufficient.

2: Transfer

(a) Study the map and the account of the development of Avonford, and then write the appropriate letters beside the names of places in the list below.

1. _____ River Exe		8. _____ Flatfields
2. _____ River Ouse		9. _____ Eighteenth-
3. _____ Roman fort		century harbour
4. _____ Saxon village		10. _____ Green Island
5. _____ British settlement		11. _____ Deeside
6. _____ Norman castle		12. _____ Brownvale
7. _____ Dog Island		13. _____ Castletown
		14. _____ Newport

(b) On the map itself, mark the location of the following by drawing the appropriate symbols: 1. bridges existing today; 2. iron ore deposits.

(c) On the map, mark with a broken line the approximate city limits of the City of Avonford as it is today.

Library work

Find out (a) when and why the Romans left Britain;

(b) who the Normans were, where they came from, and who led them in their invasion of England.

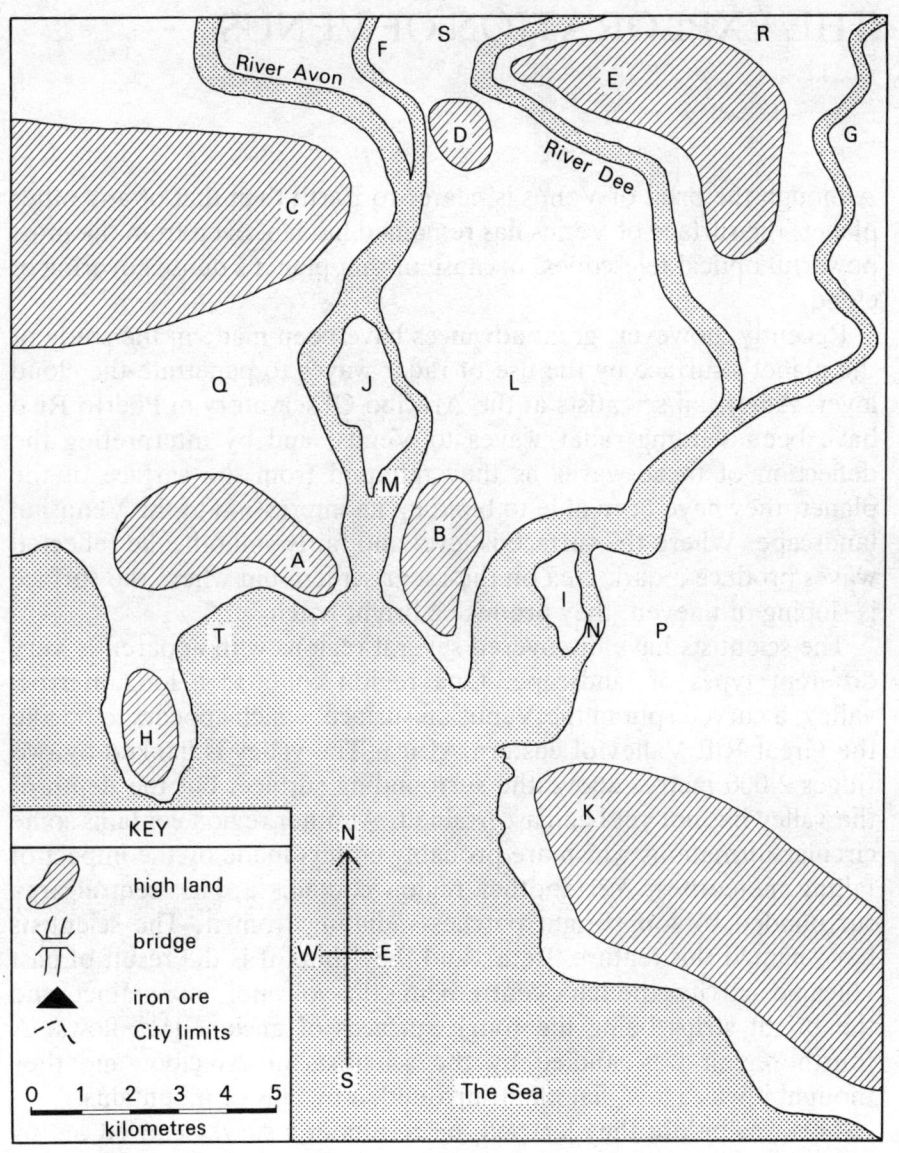

River Avon

River Dee

F S R

E

D G

C

Q J L

M

B

A

I

T N P

H

K

KEY

high land

bridge

iron ore

City limits

N

W — E

S

0 1 2 3 4 5
kilometres

The Sea

THE EXPLORATION OF VENUS

Although the orbit of Venus is nearer to Earth than that of any other planet, the surface of Venus has remained hidden, even from the most powerful optical telescopes, because of that planet's dense covering of cloud.

5   Recently, however, great advances have been made in the study of the planet's surface by the use of radar waves to penetrate the cloud layer. American scientists at the Arecibo Observatory in Puerto Rico have been sending radar waves to Venus, and by interpreting the deflection of these waves as they rebound from the surface of the

10   planet, they have been able to build up an impression of the Venusian landscape. Where the surface is level and fairly smooth, the reflected waves produce a dark area on the radar screen, but where the surface is sloping or uneven, they produce a bright patch.

The scientists have discovered several regions with apparently very

15   different types of landscape. One region contains a long, narrow valley, a curved split in the Venusian surface, which appears to be like the Great Rift Valley of eastern Africa. The valley is flanked by two ridges 2,000 metres above the surrounding surface, but the depth of the valley has not yet been ascertained. Another region contains some

20   circular formations which are probably craters made by the impact of falling meteorites. Yet another region contains a dark central area surrounded by long bright patches radiating from it. The scientists have named this feature 'Beta', and they think it is the result of past volcanic activity, the dark centre being the volcano, now extinct, and

25   the bright strips being the rough surfaces of ancient lava flows. A fourth region was studied by the scientists at Arecibo, and they thought it was a low, flat plain surrounded by hills or mountains.

This was before they learned the results of a survey carried out by the *Pioneer* spacecraft put into orbit round Venus by NASA. Like the

30   scientists at Arecibo, the NASA scientists used radar equipment, but being able to operate much closer to the planet, it could detect much greater detail than the Arecibo Observatory equipment. Furthermore, the radar equipment carried by the *Pioneer* spacecraft could be made to function in two ways: either it could produce images of the

35 Venusian landscape, or it could measure the heights and depths of different points on the surface.

It was by means of this second facility that the scientists at Arecibo were proved wrong about the fourth of the regions they had studied. Instead of a low, flat plain, the dark area turned out to be a tableland
40 about 4,000 metres high and twice as extensive as the plateau of Tibet. The existence of this tableland and the rift valley suggest that, at some stage in its history, there must have been intense pressures inside the planet, resulting in the fracture and upward movement of parts of its crust.

1: Reference

What do the following words refer to?
   (a) they (line 9)
   (b) they (line 10)
   (c) they (line 13)
   (d) This (line 28)
   (e) it (line 31)
   (f) its (line 42)

2: Understanding

Which of the following factors are mentioned in the passage as having contributed directly to the shape of the Venusian landscape?
   (a) rivers
   (b) meteorites
   (c) oceans
   (d) valleys
   (e) clouds
   (f) internal forces
   (g) volcanic action
   (h) meteorological conditions

3: Transfer

Four of the six diagrams below represent images of the Venusian surface described in the passage. Label them, using these four titles. (Two of the diagrams should be left without titles.)

1. The Rift Valley
2. The Beta Volcano
3. Meteorite craters
4. The Great Plateau

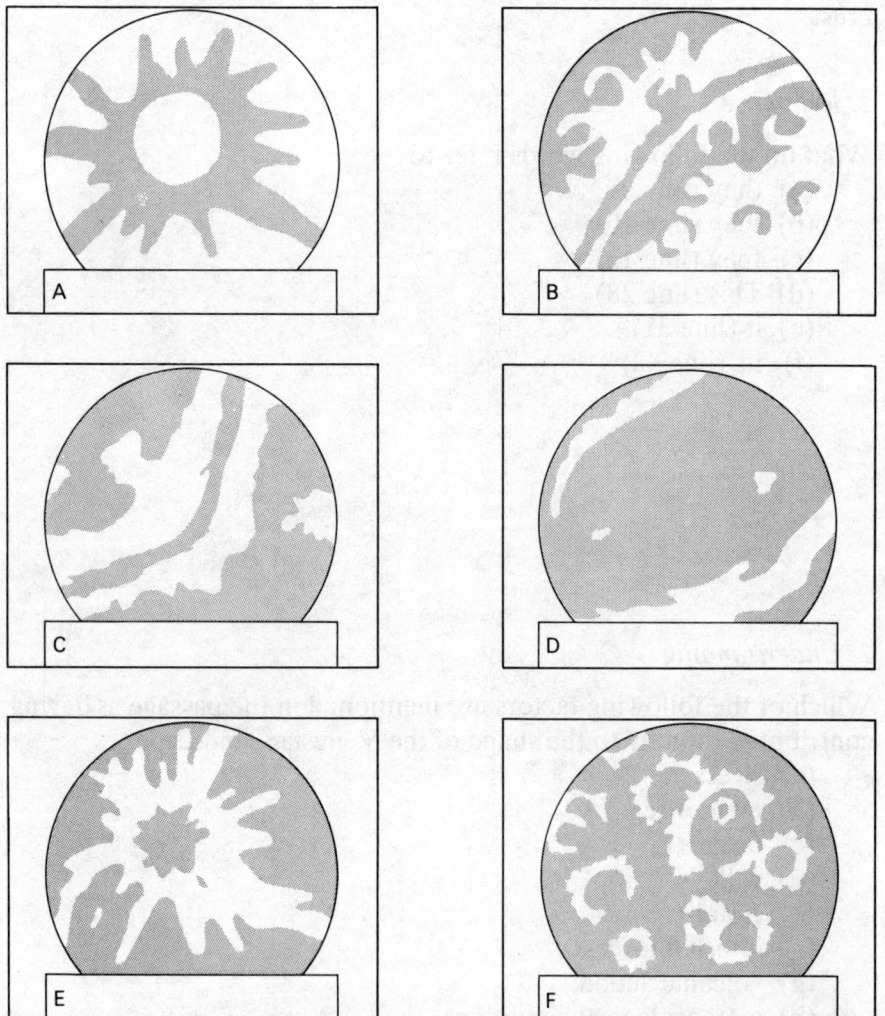

4: Composition

Use the following facts and any other facts given in the passage to write a description of Venus.

	VENUS	EARTH
Distance from Sun (million km)	107.2	148.8
Diameter (km)	12,320	12,682
Rotation on axis (earth-days)	243*	1
Orbit time (earth-days)	225	365
Moons	0	1
Mass (Earth = 1)	0.83	1
Surface atmospheric pressure (Earth = 1)	90	1
Composition of atmosphere	mainly carbon dioxide	nitrogen and oxygen
Composition of clouds	sulphuric acid droplets	water vapour
Surface temperature	+475°C	between −50°C and +50°C

*In reverse direction.

Library work

Find out (a) about the size, surface and atmosphere of Mars, and why it was thought for a long time that Mars might be inhabited;

(b) how radar works.

THE REBIRTH OF THE TOROMIRO

Easter Island in the South Pacific Ocean is famous for its huge statues, which are scattered all over the island. The people who made these statues several centuries ago seem to have had a civilisation in which the carving and erection of statues were part of an elaborate ritual. As
5   well as carving statues from stone, they also cut small faces and figures out of wood.

There was, however, only one source of wood on Easter Island, and that was the toromiro tree, which was found nowhere else in the world. At the time when the Easter Island civilisation was at its height,
10   there must have been considerable forests or plantations of the toromiro tree, but with the coming of the Europeans to the island in 1722, its fate appeared to be sealed. The Europeans who settled there in the next few decades brought sheep with them to provide food and clothing material for their survival. The grazing flocks of sheep
15   stripped the bark off the mature trees and ate the seedlings and young trees along with the other low vegetation.

By 1917, all except one toromiro tree had been killed off by the sheep. But this was not quite the end of the species, for nearly forty years later a few more trees were seen growing in isolated spots on the
20   island. In 1962, when a new search was carried out, not one living toromiro could be found, and the tree was believed to be extinct.

In 1954, however, the famous Norwegian scientist and explorer, Thor Heyerdahl, had visited Easter Island. During his stay, he had gathered some seeds from the remaining trees, and had taken them
25   back to Europe, where he had left them in the care of the Göteborg Botanic Gardens in Sweden. There the seeds lay forgotten by the outside world for a quarter of a century.

When botanists at the University of Göteborg heard in 1979 that the toromiro tree no longer grew on Easter Island, they took the 25-year-
30   old seeds and planted them in conditions as similar as possible to their native habitat. A few germinated, and now there are three precious toromiro seedlings which are being carefully nursed and guarded, so that in the not-too-distant future the toromiro tree may be found flourishing again on Easter Island.

1: Reference

What do the following words refer to?

    (a) they (line 5)
    (b) its (line 9)
    (c) its (line 12)
    (d) their (line 14)
    (e) this (line 18)
    (f) them (line 24)
    (g) they (line 29)
    (h) them (line 30)
    (i) a few (line 31)

Stone statues on Easter Island.

2: Vocabulary

Find words or phrases in the passage which could be replaced by the following without changing the meaning of the passage.

First paragraph: (a) are distributed
                   (b) religious ceremony
Second paragraph: (c) prospering
                   (d) the skin of the trunks
Third paragraph: (e) to have died out
Fourth paragraph: (f) collected
Fifth paragraph: (g) environment
                   (h) began to grow
                   (i) looked after

3: Understanding

Below are ten statements about the history of the toromiro tree. Arrange them in chronological order, and beside each write the appropriate date or period.

    A. Only one toromiro tree remained on the island.
    B. The seeds were left at a Swedish botanical garden.
    C. Several trees were found to be living on the island.
    D. A Norwegian explorer took some seeds from the island.
    E. Sheep were introduced on to Easter Island.
    F. The Easter Island people used toromiro wood for making statuettes and other objects.
    G. No living trees could be found on the island.
    H. Swedish botanists planted the seeds.
    I. The sheep destroyed the forests of toromiro trees.
    J. There are three young toromiro trees growing in Sweden.

4: Composition

Complete the list of facts shown opposite. Using this information and any information you think is relevant in the passage and the maps, write a description of Easter Island as it is today.

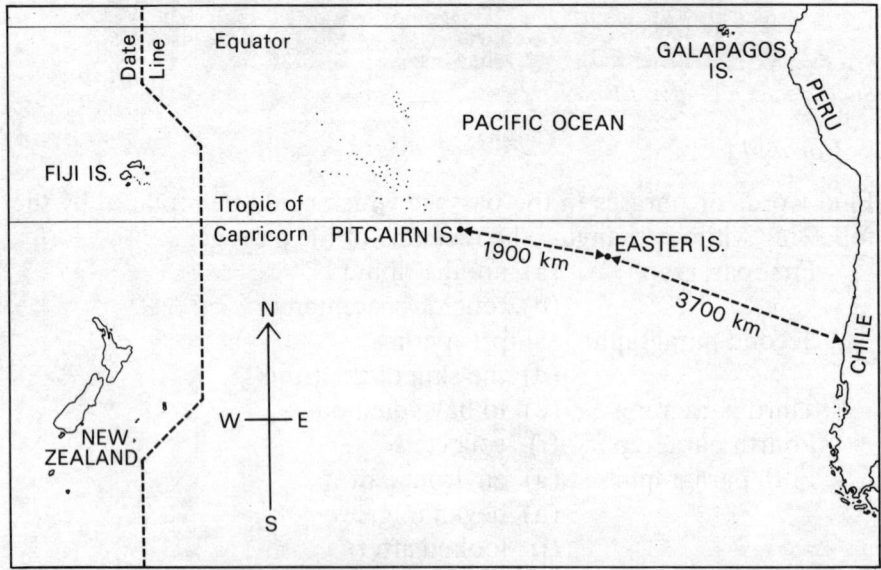

Position: _____

Shape: _____

Area: 117 sq km.

Height of highest point: _____m.

Origin: volcanic (three volcanoes, now extinct).

Surface features: no rivers; lakes in volcanic craters.

Climate: average temperatures – 25°C in January; 21°C in August;
average rainfall – 100 cm per year.

Population: about 1,000; mostly Polynesians, with a few Chilean
officials.

Administrative centre: _____

Governing country: _____

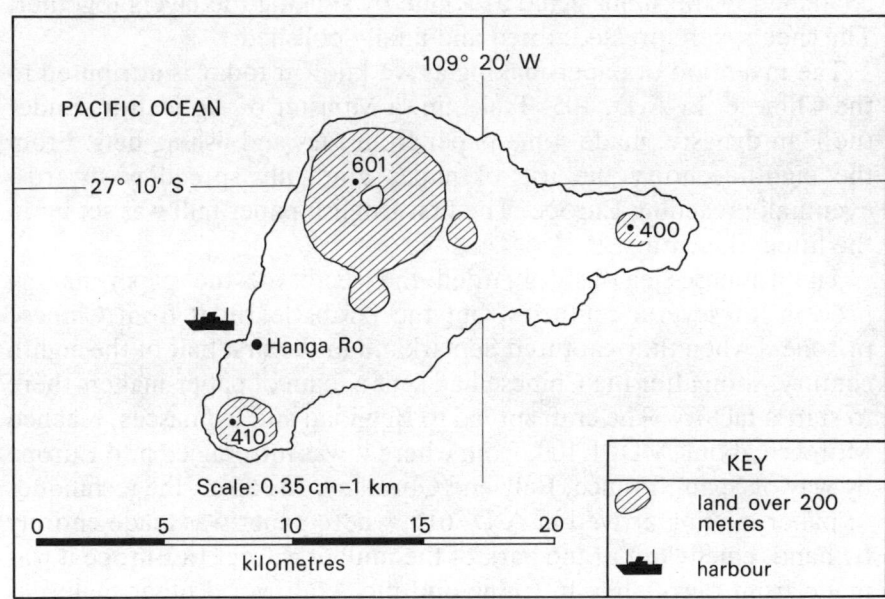

Library work

Find out about (a) the ancient culture of Easter Island;
(b) the effects of European colonisation on Easter
Island;
(c) the purposes of Thor Heyerdahl's voyages.

UNIT FOURTEEN

PAPER-MAKING

The word 'paper' is derived from a Latin word, 'papyrus', a type of writing material which was made from a water reed on the banks of the Nile and used in ancient Egypt. There is evidence that papyrus was made into sheets for writing on as early as 2,500 B.C.

5   The first man-made paper, the papyrus, was made by peeling the stems of the reed into layers with the help of a sharp tool. Several of these layers were then laid side by side, and other layers were placed crosswise on top of them. The gluten, or sticky starchy substance, contained in the stems acted as a glue by sticking the layers together.

10 The sheets were pressed, dried and finally polished.

The invention of paper-making as we know it today is attributed to the Chinese. In A.D. 105, Tsai Lun, a Minister of Agriculture under the Han dynasty, made some paper from rags and fishing nets. From the eighth century the use of paper gradually spread westwards,

15 eventually reaching Europe. The first English paper mill was set up in the fifteenth century.

The Chinese jealously guarded the secret of the paper-making process for several centuries, but the Arabs learnt it from Chinese prisoners when they captured Samarkand in the first half of the eighth

20 century, soon after the Chinese had sent a team of paper-makers there to start a factory. The craft spread to Baghdad and Damascus, reached Morocco about A.D. 1,100, from where it was introduced into Europe by way of Spain, France, Italy and Germany. In Japan, the techniques of paper-making arrived in A.D. 610, where paper was made entirely

25 by hand, chiefly out of the bark of the mulberry tree. In Europe it was made from rags, while in China and the Arab world other materials were used as well as rags.

Even in the early days, paper was probably made in much the same way as today. The bark or other fibrous material was prepared by

30 pounding. The Japanese, however, boiled the mulberry wood first so that the bark could be removed more easily, and then they scraped and washed the bark before pounding it into pulp. A common practice, carried out by the Japanese, the Arabs and other paper-makers, was boiling the fibrous raw material with lime to break it down. When the

35 Arabs used rags, they found that if they soaked them thoroughly and

left them to ferment, the resulting partially rotten mass could be
reduced to pulp more easily.

In 1710, a different method of preparing the fibrous material was
developed in Holland. A machine was invented which consisted of a
40   bedplate, over which revolved a cylinder with blades projecting from
it. As it turned, the blades shredded the material on the bedplate into
fibres.

The preparation of paper from the pulp was a process of shaping the
pulp into sheets and then drying them. The moulds into which the pulp
45   was poured were usually wooden frames with cloth stretched across
the bottom through which the water drained out of the pulp. Later,
wire mesh was used instead of cloth. Another way was to dip the frame
into a vat of pulp and lift it out with an agitating motion so that the
draining pulp was distributed evenly.
50   In 1798, the Frenchman Louis Robert invented a method of
paper-making by which sheets up to 3 metres wide and 16 metres long
could be made. The pulp was poured on to a wire mesh conveyor belt,
where it drained before passing between rollers which squeezed out
the remaining water and produced sheets of uniform thinness. Modern
55   machines are based on the same principle.

1: Reference

What do the following words and phrases refer to?
- (a) them (line 8)
- (b) it (line 11)
- (c) it (line 18)
- (d) there (line 20)
- (e) The craft (line 21)
- (f) it (line 25)
- (g) them (line 35)
- (h) it (line 48)
- (i) the same principle (line 55)

2: Understanding

Of the ten sentences below, some are true according to the passage, and some are false. Write T beside those which are true, and F beside those which are false.

_____ 1. Paper was being made over 4,000 years ago.

_____ 2. The Japanese were making paper before the Europeans.

_____ 3. When paper-making started in Japan, Chinese machinery was used.

_____ 4. Lime was used in paper-making to make the paper dry quickly.

_____ 5. The Japanese heated mulberry wood in water to break it down into pulp.

_____ 6. Modern paper-making follows the same principle as that employed by Louis Robert's machinery.

_____ 7. The French invention at the end of the eighteenth century allowed the production of paper in very large sizes.

_____ 8. Paper-making entered Europe from Morocco.

_____ 9. The Arabs were making paper before the Japanese.

_____ 10. A sharp tool was used for peeling the stems of the papyrus reed.

3: Transfer

In the table below, indicate with a tick (√) which processes in the manufacture of paper were used by which peoples.

	Egyptians	Chinese	Japanese	Arabs	Europeans
Peeling off layers					
Separating bark by boiling					
Pounding					
Boiling with lime					
Fermentation of rags					
Shredding					
Scraping and washing of the bark					

4: Transfer

In the boxes on the map, write the date when the craft of paper-making first started in each of the places indicated.

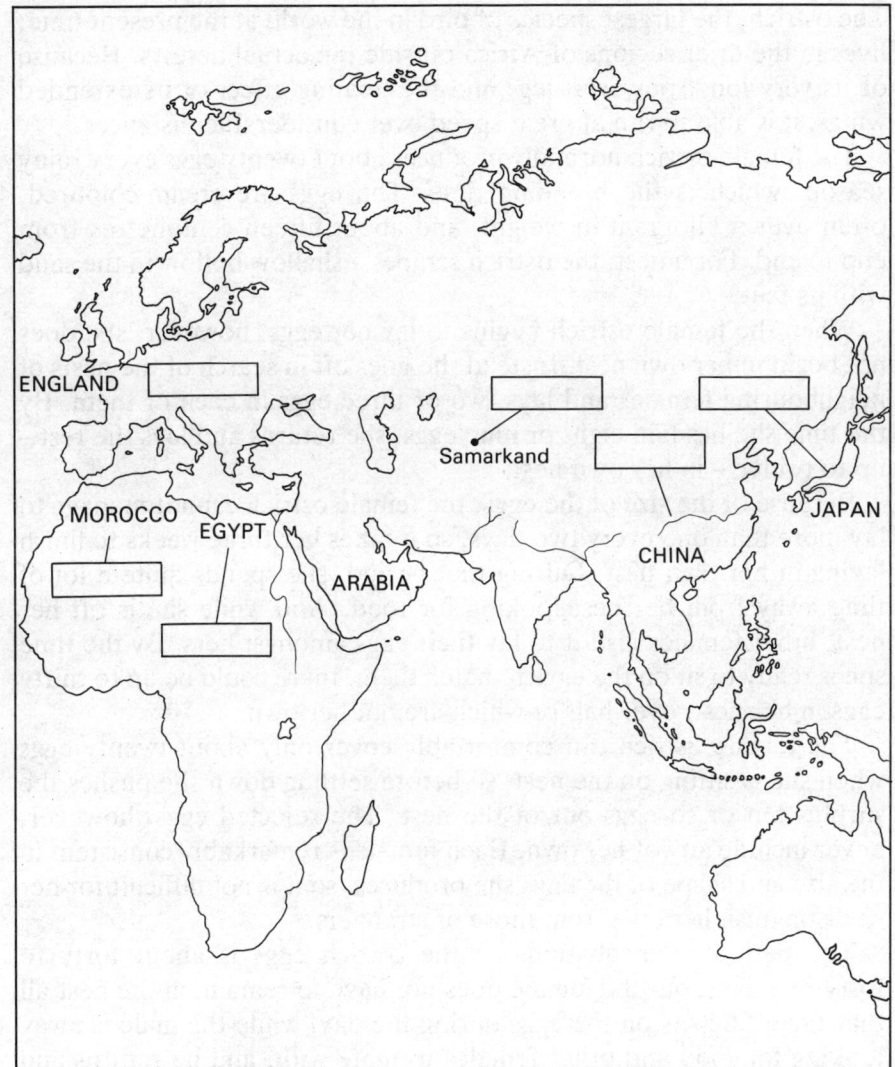

Library work

Find out by what process paper is made not to absorb ink.

OSTRICHES AND THEIR EGGS

The ostrich, the largest species of bird in the world at the present time, lives in the drier regions of Africa outside the actual deserts. Because of its very long, powerful legs and the floating effect of its extended wings, it is able to run at great speed over considerable distances.

5 The female ostrich normally produces about twenty eggs every rainy season, which is the breeding time. The eggs are cream-coloured, often over a kilogram in weight, and about fifteen centimetres from end to end. For a nest, the ostrich scrapes a shallow hollow in the sand with its feet.

10 When the female ostrich begins to lay her eggs, however, she does not begin in her own nest. Instead she goes off in search of the nests of neighbouring females and lays two or three eggs in each of them. By the time she has laid eight or nine eggs, she returns and lays the rest – up to twelve – in her own nest.

15 Because of the size of the eggs, the female ostrich cannot manage to lay more than one every two days, so it takes her three weeks to finish laying in her own nest. During that period, she spends quite a lot of time away from her nest looking for food. And while she is off her nest, other females visit it to lay their eggs amongst hers. By the time 20 she is ready to sit on the eggs to hatch them, there could be up to thirty eggs in her nest, over half of which are not her own.

The female ostrich can comfortably cover only about twenty eggs when she is sitting on the nest, so before settling down she pushes the surplus ten or so eggs out of the nest. The rejected eggs, however, 25 never include any of her own. Each female is remarkably consistent in the size and shape of the eggs she produces, so it is not difficult for her to distinguish her own from those of strangers.

The period of incubation for the ostrich eggs is about forty to forty-two days, but the female does not have to remain on the nest all 30 that time. She sits on the eggs during the day, while the male is away looking for food and other females to mate with, and he returns and sits through the night so that the female can go in search of food.

Of all the eggs laid by a colony of ostriches, only a very small number hatch into young birds. There are, of necessity, times when 35 nests are left unprotected, for there are too few males to sit on all the

nests at night. Thus there are ample opportunities for predators to raid the nests and break open and eat the eggs. In fact, nearly 80% of the nests are destroyed. But even if a particular female's nest suffers this fate, there is a good chance that one or two of her eggs will be hatched
40 in the nest of one of her neighbours.

1: Reference

What do the following words refer to?
    (a) it (line 4)
    (b) she (line 13)
    (c) it (line 16)
    (d) it (line 26)
    (e) those (line 27)
    (f) he (line 31)
    (g) this fate (lines 38-9)

2: Vocabulary

Find words or phrases in the passage which could be replaced by the following without changing the meaning of the passage.

First paragraph:	(a)	spread
Second paragraph:	(b)	long
	(c)	digs
Fifth paragraph:	(d)	extra
	(e)	abandoned
	(f)	regular
	(g)	pick out
Sixth paragraph:	(h)	keeping the eggs at an even temperature
Seventh paragraph:	(i)	break open and produce
	(j)	plenty of
	(k)	other animals in search of food

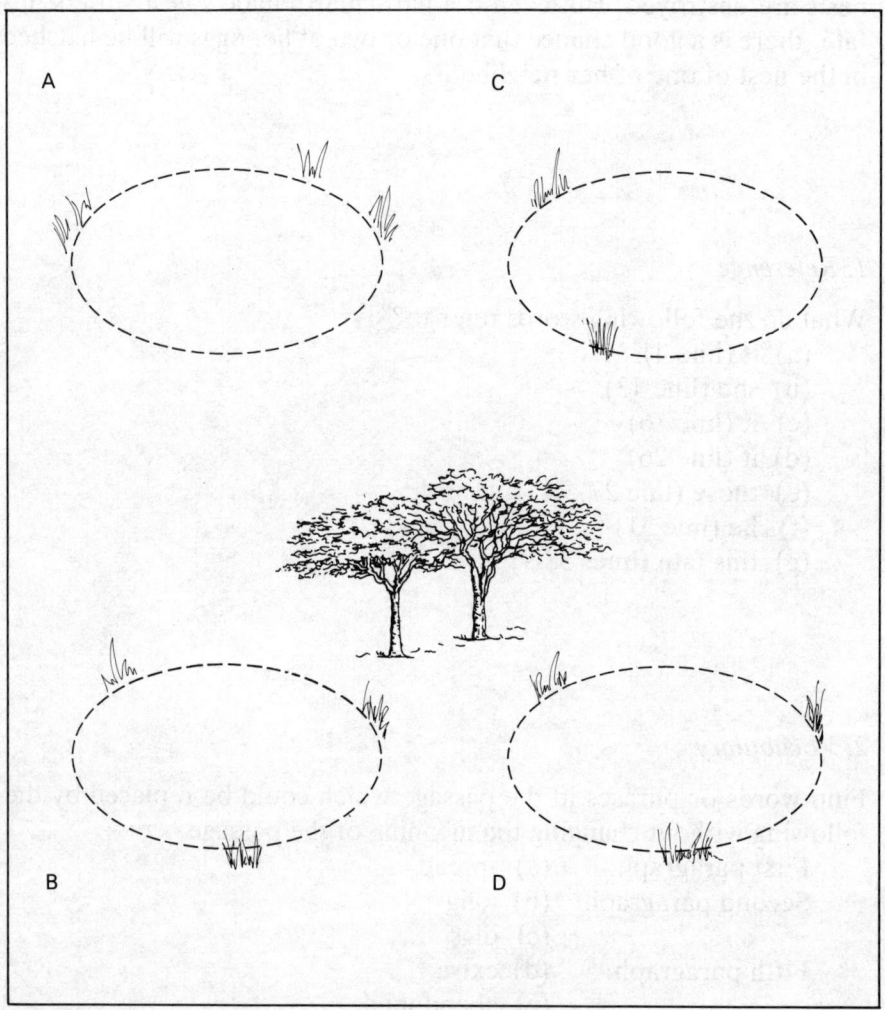

In the diagram above there are four empty nests. A certain female ostrich, called Olivia, has made nest A, and nests B, C and D have been made by three other female ostriches. Olivia lays twenty eggs altogether. Show where she is likely to lay them, by writing the numbers 1 to 20 in the nests in the diagram. Write the number 1 for the first egg she lays, 2 for the second egg, 3 for the third egg, and so on. (There are several possible correct answers.)

4: Transfer

Below are three diagrams showing an ostrich's nest at different stages during the breeding season. One diagram shows the nest thirty days after the ostrich started laying, another shows the nest as the ostrich is about to start incubation (approximately the fortieth day), and the third shows the nest in the middle of the incubation period (approximately the sixtieth day).

(a) Label the diagrams '30 days', '40 days', and '60 days'.

(b) The owner of this nest lays twenty eggs in all, of which she lays twelve in her own nest. On each of the diagrams, mark with a cross (X) the eggs which could be her own.

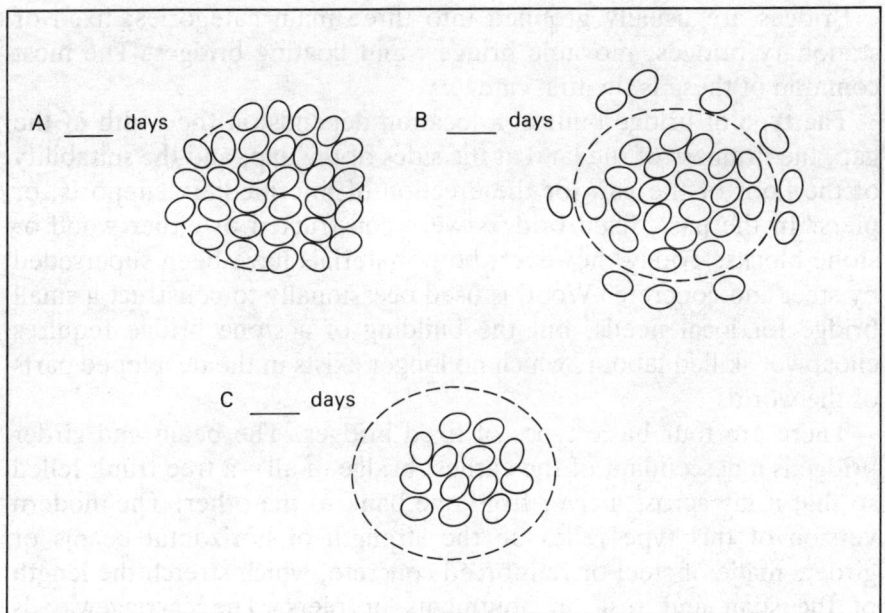

A _____ days

B _____ days

C _____ days

Library work

Find out (a) the average size and weight of an adult ostrich;

(b) more precisely than it tells you in the passage, in which continents and countries ostriches can be found;

(c) about living and recently extinct relatives of the ostrich, and where they live or lived.

UNIT SIXTEEN

FIXED BRIDGES

It is not surprising that Man's need to transport himself or his commodities across a gap has given rise to a wide variety of types of bridges. Simple bridges consist of a single span supported at each end by abutments. Others have two or more spans, with a pier between
5   each pair of spans; and we may call these composite, or continuous, bridges. Some bridges have the carriageway built on top of the main structure of the bridge. These are called deck bridges. Others, through bridges, have essential parts of the structure extending above the carriageway.
10   Bridges are usually grouped into three main categories; fixed or stationary bridges, movable bridges, and floating bridges. The most common of these is the first category.

The type of bridge built in a location depends on the width of the gap, the firmness of the land at the sides of the gap, and the suitability
15   of the floor of the gap for the erection of intermediary supports, or piers. In the past, fixed bridges were constructed of either wood or stone blocks. Today, however, both materials have been superseded by steel and concrete. Wood is used occasionally to construct a small bridge for local needs, but the building of a stone bridge requires
20   cheap yet skilled labour, which no longer exists in the developed parts of the world.

There are four basic types of fixed bridges. The beam and girder bridge is a descendant of the earliest bridge of all – a tree trunk felled so that it lay across a river from one bank to the other. The modern
25   version of this type relies on the strength of horizontal beams or girders made of steel or reinforced concrete, which stretch the length of the span and rest on abutments or piers. The carriageway is constructed on the top surface of the beams.

The simple truss bridge consists of two steel frames, or trusses, one
30   on each side of the carriageway, joined top and bottom by cross-members. A truss is in the form of a series of triangles. The top horizontal members are called the upper chord. This is joined to the lower chord by vertical and diagonal members which comprise the web system. On the cross-members between the lower chords of the two
35   trusses is constructed the carriageway. A variation of the truss bridge

is the cantilever bridge. In this type there are two truss structures each supported by a central pier. One end of each structure is anchored to an abutment on the bank, while the other ends are connected by a structure known as a suspended span.

40   The arch bridge has a very long history. Examples of this type were built of stone in ancient Mesopotamia, Egypt and China, and the Romans excelled in its construction. Composite arch bridges such as those built to carry railways or canals in nineteenth-century Britain are called viaducts or aqueducts respectively. Nowadays, arch bridges are

45   built of concrete or steel. The carriageway is normally laid down over the top of the arch, but there are some examples of this type where the middle stretch is suspended beneath the highest part of the arch.

The fourth type of fixed bridge is the suspension bridge. It is given this name because the carriageway is suspended on cables from two

50   high towers, one on each side of the river. This type of bridge is used over wide stretches of water where intermediary piers cannot be built. The towers may be built of concrete or steel, and the long structure bearing the carriageway is made of steel girders.

1: Understanding

Which of the following statements are true and which are false?
 1. The Romans were skilled at building arch bridges.
 2. A continuous bridge is a bridge which has only one span.
 3. Viaducts were built in nineteenth-century England to carry canals.
 4. A composite bridge is a bridge which has important parts of its structure above the level of the carriageway.
 5. The web system holds together the upper and lower chords of a truss.
 6. A deck bridge is a bridge which supports the carriageway entirely from beneath.
 7. There is no longer any skilled labour in the developed parts of the world.
 8. A through bridge is a bridge which is made up of several spans supported at intervals by piers.
 9. The suspended span is a part of a suspension bridge.
10. The cantilever bridge is a type of truss bridge.

2: Transfer

Complete the table about modern fixed bridges, listing them in alphabetical order. You should leave no blank spaces in the table.

TYPE OF BRIDGE	MATERIALS USED	THROUGH/DECK

3: Transfer

(a) In the spaces under the diagrams, write the names of the bridges illustrated. Write X if the bridge is not mentioned in the passage.
(b) Study the passage and the key to the diagrams, and then write the appropriate letters in the circles on diagrams 1, 2 and 3.

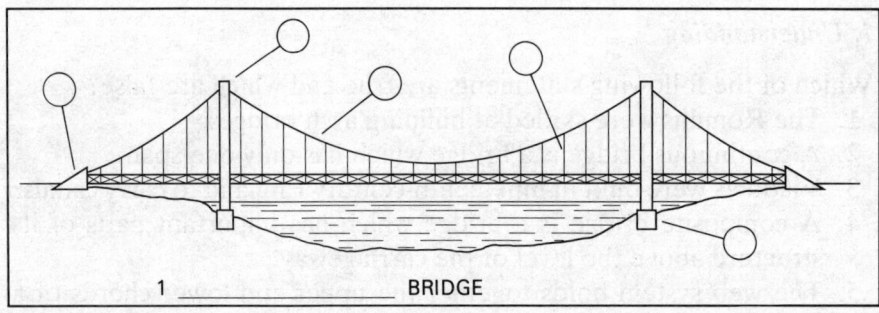

1 _____ BRIDGE

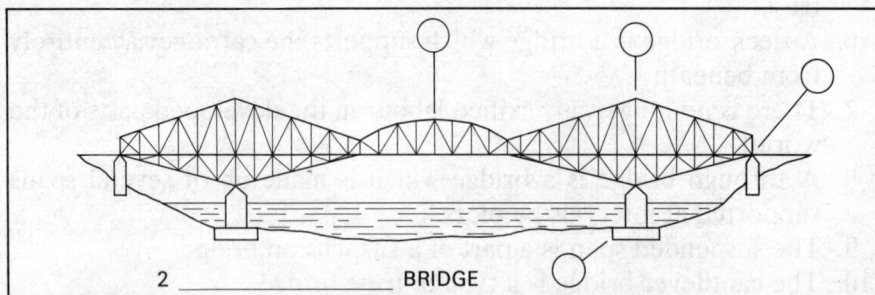

2 _____ BRIDGE

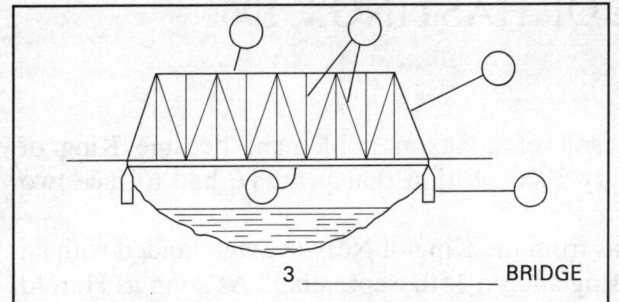

3 _____ BRIDGE

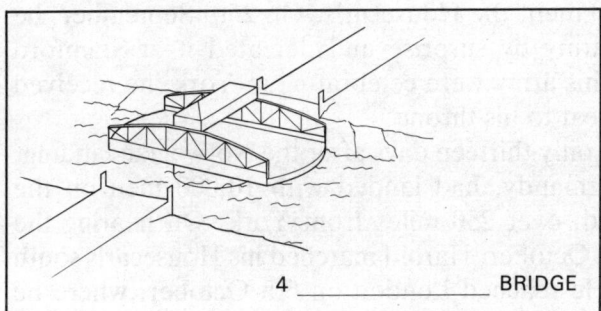

4 _____ BRIDGE

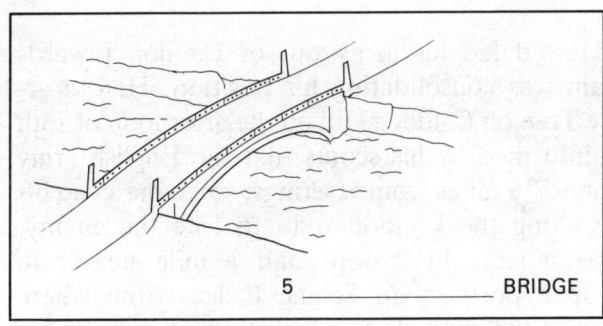

5 _____ BRIDGE

KEY

A. abutment
B. lower chord
C. main cable
D. pier
E. suspended span
F. suspender
G. tower
H. truss structure
I. upper chord
J. web system

Library work

Find out about the following:
  (a) the length, type and age of the longest bridge in the world;
  (b) the length, type and age of the longest bridge in your own country or region of the world;
  (c) The Golden Gate bridge, San Francisco, U.S.A.;
  (d) Tower Bridge, London;
  (e) Sydney Harbour Bridge, Australia;
  (f) 'Galloping Gertie' bridge, U.S.A.

THE BATTLE OF HASTINGS, 1066

Harold Godwin, the son of a Saxon nobleman, became King of England on 6th January 1066. Within that year, he had to face two threats to his throne.

5 The first of these was from the King of Norway, who landed with an army in the north of England on 15th September. As soon as Harold heard of this, he marched north at great speed with his highly trained personal army of 3,000 men, the Housecarls. On 25th September, he took the Norwegian army by surprise and defeated it at Stamford Bridge. While he and his army were celebrating in York, he received
10 word of the second threat to his throne.

On 28th September, only thirteen days after the Norwegian landing, William, Duke of Normandy, had landed with 10,000 men on the south coast of England, over 250 miles from York. On hearing the news, which was on 1st October, Harold marched his Housecarls south
15 to confront William. He reached London on 6th October, where he remained for five days collecting what men he could to supplement the Housecarls.

On the sixth day, Harold led his army out of London towards Hastings, where William was consolidating his position. Harold ar-
20 rived at the Hoar Apple Tree on Caldbec Hill on the afternoon of 13th October. William was informed by his scouts that the English army had arrived and were only 7½ miles from Hastings, so he marched his army out of the town along the London road to face the enemy. Meanwhile Harold was moving his troops half a mile nearer to
25 Hastings. They took up a position on Senlac Ridge, from where Harold had a good view of the road along which William's army was advancing.

William's army camped for the night on Telham Hill, from where he could observe the English army half a mile away up the road. At dawn
30 the next day, William's army prepared to attack. They marched forward and took up positions on the southern slope of the ridge in three divisions.

In the centre, stretching westwards from the road and across the head of a marshy valley was the main force of over 4,000 men, the
35 Normans, commanded by William himself. On the right, to the east of

the road and standing between the village of Senlac and the English army, was the Franco-Flemish division of about 2,000 men. And on the left was the smallest of the divisions, the Bretons. They were in a rather dangerous situation, for behind them beyond a wooden hill was
40 a marsh in the bottom of a valley.

The army they were facing was also made up of three divisions. In the centre, straddling the road and protecting Harold's command post on the highest point of the ridge was the division of Housecarls. After the Battle of Stamford Bridge and their long marches, their numerical
45 strength must have been well below 3,000, and they were now supplemented by a large number of occasional soldiers, the Fyrd. The two divisions on either side of the centre were composed mainly of the Fyrd. The total strength of Harold's army was between 8,000 and 9,000 men, who were stretched out along the whole length of the
50 ridge, apart for a small number of Housecarls who were guarding their king at the command post.

The invading army began their attack on the English positions at about 9 a.m. The battle raged fiercely for eight hours, during which time both armies suffered heavy losses, until finally Harold was killed
55 and the remnants of his army fled in confusion and despair.

1: Reference

What do the following words refer to?
(a) these (line 4)
(b) this (line 6)
(c) he (line 7)
(d) he (line 15)
(e) he (line 22)
(f) They (line 25)
(g) They (line 30)
(h) They (line 38)
(i) they (line 45)

2: Vocabulary

Find words or phrases in the passage which could be replaced by the following without changing the meaning of the passage.

First paragraph:	(a)	lord
Second paragraph:	(b)	challenge to
Fourth paragraph:	(c)	establishing a base
	(d)	spies
Sixth paragraph:	(e)	an area of very wet ground
Seventh paragraph:	(f)	stretching across
	(g)	supported
	(h)	part-time
Eighth paragraph:	(i)	many soldiers were killed
	(j)	remains

3: Understanding

Arrange the following fourteen statements in their correct chronological order, and write the appropriate date beside each.

1. William took his army out of Hastings to confront Harold.
2. The English army camped on Senlac Ridge.
3. Harold and his Housecarls celebrated their victory in York.
4. The King of Norway landed in northern England with an army.
5. The Norwegians were defeated at the Battle of Stamford Bridge.
6. The news of William's landing reached Harold in York.
7. Harold stayed in London for a few days building up his army.
8. The English army reached Caldbec Hill.
9. William marched his troops towards Senlac Ridge.
10. The Norman army camped on Telham Hill.
11. Harold left London with his strengthened army in the direction of the south coast.
12. Harold marched back to London.
13. Harold marched north with his Housecarls to confront the Norwegian army.
14. William of Normandy landed in southern England with an army.

(a) On the map, mark the following:
  (i) the Hoar Apple Tree, with the letter A;
  (ii) Harold's command post, with the letter H;
  (iii) William's command post, with the letter W.
(b) Draw block shapes (▢) to show the positions of the three divisions of William's army at 9 a.m. on the day of the battle, labelling them N (Norman), B (Breton), and F (Franco-Flemish) respectively.
(c) Fill in the blank spaces in the key.

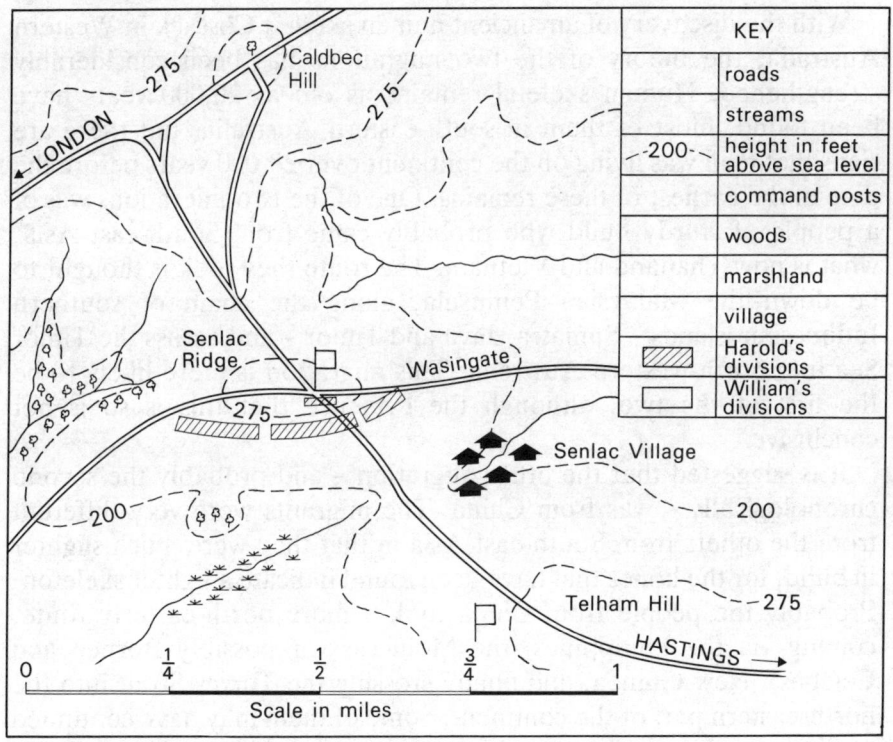

Library work

(a) Find out what parts Harold's brothers played in the events of 1066.
(b) Prepare a five minute talk on how and why William defeated Harold at the Battle of Hastings.

THE FIRST AUSTRALIANS

Various theories have been put forward about how and when man came to Australia in prehistoric times. Until recently, two theories seemed particularly plausible. One of these was that there was one major migration, probably from China or South-east Asia via the Indonesian archipelago, followed by three relatively small-scale colonisations. The other theory was that there were two separate migrations, each of a different human type.

With the discovery of an ancient human skull at Cossack in Western Australia, the theory of the two migrations has been considerably strengthened. Human skeletal remains as old as 26,000 years have been found, most of them in south-eastern Australia, but there are signs that man was living on the continent over 20,000 years before the date of the earliest of these remains. One of the two migrations was of a people of sturdy build who probably came from South-east Asia, what is now Thailand and Vietnam. The route they took is thought to be down the Malaysian Peninsula, along the chain of southern Indonesian islands – Sumatra, Java and Timor – and across the Timor Sea into north-western Australia. This migration is more likely to be the first of the two, although the evidence that this is so is not conclusive.

It is suggested that the other migration – and probably the second chronologically – was from China. The migrants were very different from the others from South-east Asia in that they were much slighter in build, for the bones that have been found indicate a lighter skeleton. Probably the people from China took a more north-easterly route, coming via the Philippines, the Moluccas (or possibly Borneo and Celebes), New Guinea, and finally crossing the Torres Strait into the north-eastern part of the continent. Some of them may have continued south down the east coast and into Tasmania, which at that time was joined to the Australian mainland. Both these waves of migration must have taken place at times when the polar icecaps were considerably more extensive and consequently the sea level was much lower than today, so that many of the Indonesian islands would have been joined together.

35   Over the thousands of years following these migrations, the two peoples that had inhabited the continent became mixed, resulting in the Australian Aborigine of today, who shows traces of the characteristics of both peoples.

1: Reference

What do the following words and phrases refer to?
  (a) One (line 3)
  (b) each (line 7)
  (c) most of them (line 11)
  (d) the two (line 19)
  (e) this is so (line 19)
  (f) It (line 21)
  (g) they (line 23)
  (h) them (line 28)

Australian Aborigines performing a kangaroo dance.

2: Transfer

Look at the map of South-east Asia and Australia.

    (a) Write the correct letters in the spaces in the map. Refer to the key.

    (b) Draw the two possible alternatives for the route of the migration from China, and the route of the migration from South-east Asia. Use the symbols in the key.

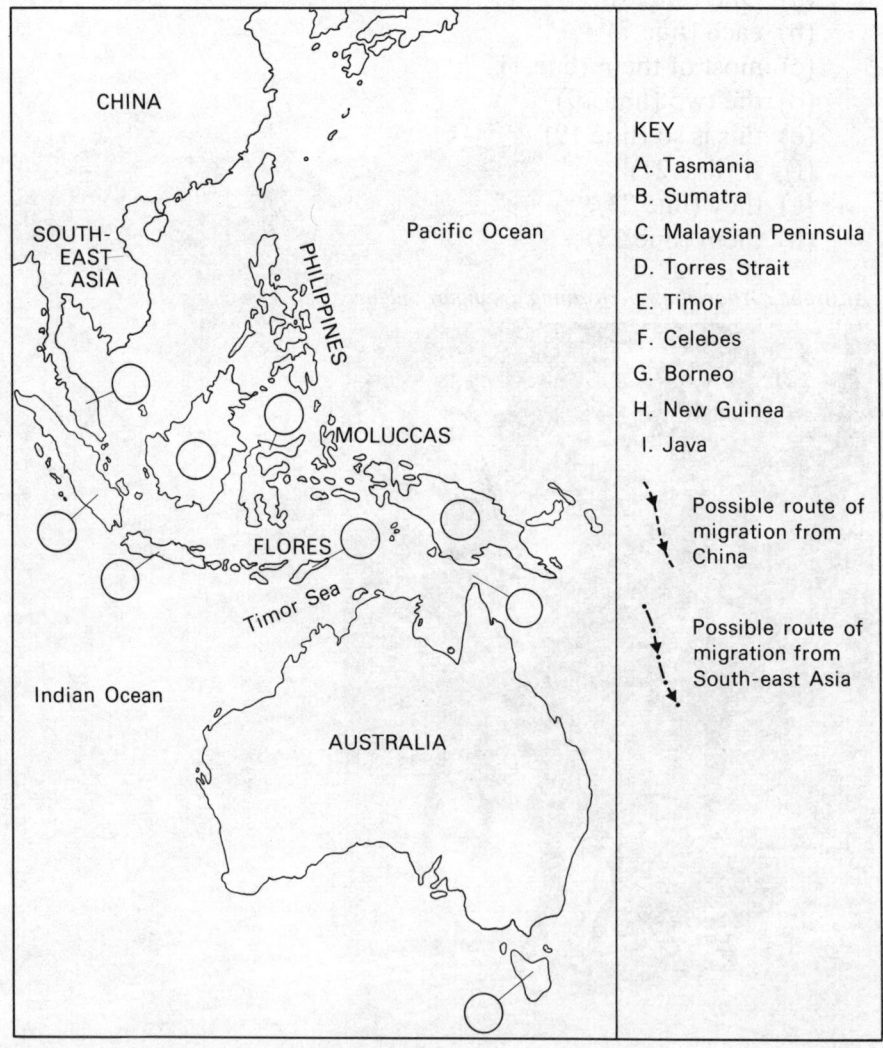

KEY

A. Tasmania

B. Sumatra

C. Malaysian Peninsula

D. Torres Strait

E. Timor

F. Celebes

G. Borneo

H. New Guinea

I. Java

Possible route of migration from China

Possible route of migration from South-east Asia

3: Transfer

Complete the table below.

	FIRST MIGRATION	SECOND MIGRATION
Build of people		
Area of origin		
Two places on route 1.		
2.		
Area of arrival		

4: Understanding

Which of the following statements are true according to the passage?

1. Pieces of human skeleton over 20,000 years old have been found in Australia.
2. The people of sturdy build came from South-east Asia.
3. Some people found their way into Tasmania.
4. The people of slighter build passed through the Philippines and New Guinea.
5. In prehistoric times, people arrived in Australia from the north.
6. One of the migrations came across the Timor Sea.
7. A prehistoric human skull has been found at Cossack, Western Australia.
8. The second migration to Australia was from China.
9. The bones of two types of prehistoric people have been found in Australia.
10. The people originating in China had light bones.

Library work

Find out (a) about the traditional way of life of the Australian Aborigines;

(b) how the Tasmanians were wiped out in the nineteenth century.

UNIT NINETEEN

EARLY DEVELOPMENTS IN STEAM POWER

Steam power was one of the main factors in the industrial revolution that took place in Britain roughly between 1760 and 1830. The first steam engine to be used industrially, however, was the one invented by Thomas Savery towards the end of the seventeenth century.

5   In 1698 Thomas Savery patented his steam engine, which was being used to pump floodwater out of copper mines in south-western England. Savery had got his ideas for the engine from inventors in Europe. In 1654, Otto von Guericke developed a vacuum pump, which inspired a Frenchman, Denis Papir, in 1695 to construct a piston

10 pump, exploiting first the force of the explosion of gunpowder and later steam power to operate a piston. Savery, however, did not adopt the idea of having a piston. Instead, he had the steam from a boiler passing directly into a 'receiver', or condensing tank, by means of a short horizontal pipe. The receiver was connected in turn with the

15 floodwater in the mine by another short horizontal pipe leading into a long vertical pipe which extended from the floor of the flooded chamber to the surface at the top of the mine.

   When the receiver had filled up with steam, cold water was sprayed on to the outside of the receiver from a pipe above, and as the steam

20 condensed a vacuum was created inside the receiver, and this vacuum sucked the floodwater up the vertical pipe and out of the mine. Some water, of course, was sucked into the bottom of the receiver, but because the diameter of the tank was so much greater than that of the vertical pipe the former filled very slowly.

25 Savery's engine could not pump water higher than about thirty metres. To do so would generate so much pressure inside the boiler that it would burst. It was not long, therefore, before it was super-seded in mine drainage by a more efficient system.

   Thomas Newcomen revived the idea of the piston which Savery had

30 eschewed. In 1706 he developed a steam engine which rapidly replaced Savery's pump in the mining industry. From the boiler, the steam passed straight up into a cylinder which housed a piston. The piston was connected by a chain to one end of a rocker-beam, hanging from the other end of which was a counter-weight. The piston was forced up

35 the cylinder by the pressure of the steam assisted by the pull of the

counter-weight at the other end of the rocker-beam. When the piston reached the top of its stroke, water was admitted into the bottom of the cylinder to cause condensation, and the vacuum thus created caused the piston to be drawn back down the cylinder. In this way a rocking motion was set up which operated a pumping mechanism.

40

1: Reference

What do the following words and phrases refer to?
- (a) one (line 3)
- (b) inventors (line 7)
- (c) condensing tank (line 13)
- (d) that (line 23)
- (e) the former (line 24)
- (f) To do so (line 26)
- (g) which (line 34)

The Savery-Newcomen Steam Engine of 1712.

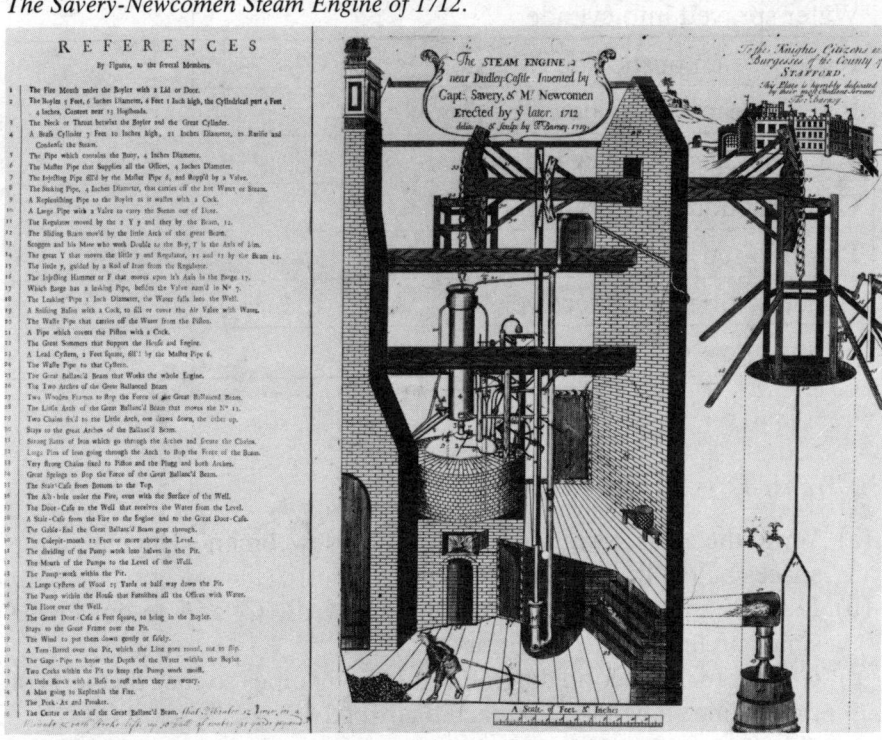

2: Transfer

There are five stages in the operation of Savery's engine, and ten in the operation of Newcomen's. In the table below, the stages are not in the correct order. Show the correct order by writing the numbers 1 to 5 in the column headed 'Savery's Engine', and the numbers 1 to 10 in the column headed 'Newcomen's Engine'.

STAGES IN OPERATION	SAVERY'S ENGINE	NEWCOMEN'S ENGINE
Boiler heated		
Piston falls		
Pump completes one cycle		
Floodwater expelled		
Steam enters receiver		
Water sprayed into cylinder		
Rocker-beam pushed up by piston		
Rocker-beam pulled down by piston		
Water sprayed on to cylinder		
Condensation inside cylinder		
Piston raised		
Condensation inside receiver		
Steam enters cylinder		

3: Transfer

(a) Write the titles 'Savery's Engine' and 'Newcomen's Engine' in the spaces below the two diagrams.
(b) Label the parts by writing the letters A, B, C, and so on, in the small circles in both diagrams.
(c) Complete the second diagram by drawing pipes so that the parts of the engine shown are connected correctly.

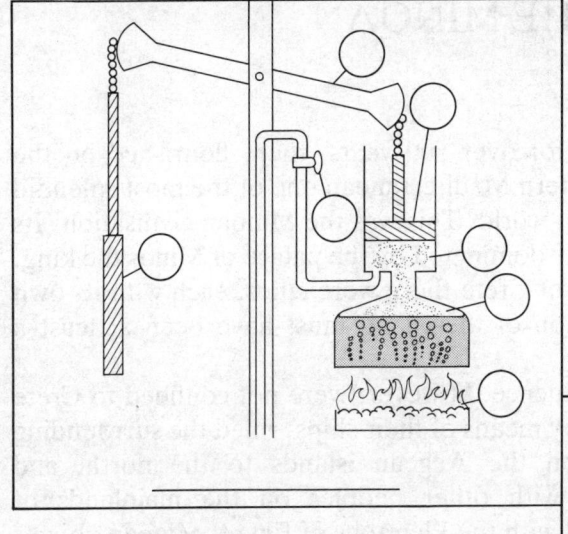

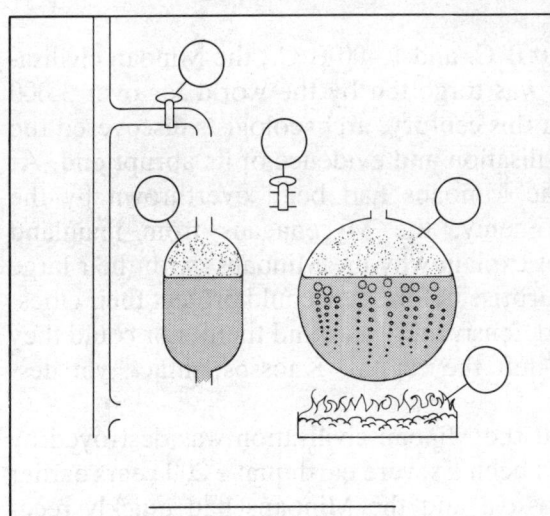

KEY

A. tap
B. boiler
C. piston
D. fire
E. counter-weight
F. condensing tank
G. cylinder
H. rocker-beam

Library work

Find out about (a) James Watt's improvements to Newcomen's engine;

(b) the development of the steam locomotive.

THE END OF THE MINOAN CIVILISATION

From about 2,000 B.C. for over 500 years, there flourished on the island of Crete in the eastern Mediterranean one of the most splendid civilisations of the ancient world. This was the Minoan civilisation. Its capital was Knossos, a city dominated by the palace of Minos the king.
5   All over the eastern half of Crete there were cities, each with its own palace, and the population of the island must have been at least a quarter of a million.

Minoan power and influence, however, were not confined to Crete alone, for the Minoans, by means of their ships, ruled the surrounding
10   seas, set up colonies on the Aegean islands to the north, and established trade links with other peoples on the mainlands of Anatolia and Greece and with the Pharaohs of Egypt. Minoan objects and cultural influence have been found, for example, in the ruins of Mycenae in Greece.

15   Suddenly, between 1,500 B.C. and 1,400 B.C., the Minoan civilisation came to an end, and was forgotten by the world for over 3,000 years. In the early years of this century, archaeologists discovered the remains of the Minoan civilisation and evidence of its abrupt end. At first they thought that the Minoans had been overthrown by the
20   invasion of a powerful enemy, the Mycenaeans from mainland Greece, but they could not explain why the Minoans, with their large fleet, should be taken by surprise before they could protect their cities, for there were no signs of defensive walls around them; nor could they explain why the invaders left the capital, Knossos, intact, yet des-
25   troyed all the other cities.

Another theory was that the Minoan civilisation was destroyed by earthquakes. But there had been a severe earthquake 200 years earlier which had destroyed Knossos, and the Minoans had quickly recovered. It was not until the results of excavations on Thera, an island
30   100 kilometres north of Crete, became known that another theory began to be taken seriously.

Thera is a volcanic island. Geologists have established that it has been shattered by two massive explosions in the last 25,000 years. At one time, Thera was a volcanic cone. The first explosion it suffered
35   blew the top off, leaving a caldera. The sea entered through the gaps in

the ring of cliffs surrounding the caldera and flooded it. During the
thousands of years since the explosion of 23,000 B.C. pressure built up
beneath the caldera, relieved from time to time by eruptions which
formed small cones.

40   In about 1,500 B.C. Thera entered into another phase of intense
volcanic activity. Enormous quantities of tephra were thrown out on to
the edges of the caldera, which at that time was the site of a thriving
Minoan colony. The inhabitants fled. The volcano then went into a
phase of subdued activity for about thirty years, at the end of which it
45   exploded with a violence never witnessed before or since by civilised
man.

The effects were catastrophic. This time the tephra was ejected
much higher into the atmosphere, where it spread out and fell over a
wide area stretching from central Crete nearly as far as Cyprus 600
50   kilometres to the east. And as the floor of the caldera collapsed,
tsunamis raced in ever-widening circles to devastate the coasts of
Greece, Anatolia, and Crete.

Thus was the Minoan civilisation destroyed. Most of its cities, being
on the coast, were flattened by the tsunamis, and the people who
55   escaped the deluge found themselves facing starvation, for their crops
lay under a thick blanket of tephra. Knossos, standing on a hill out of
reach of the tsunamis, was undamaged, but it was now like a head
without a body, and within a very few years it was in the hands of the
Mycenaeans.

1: Reference

What do the following words and phrases refer to?
   (a) This (line 3)
   (b) they (line 21)
   (c) the invaders (line 24)
   (d) earlier (than when?) (line 27)
   (e) it (line 36)
   (f) to the east (of where?) (line 50)
   (g) themselves (line 55)
   (h) within a very few years (of when?) (line 58)
   (i) it (line 58)

2: Vocabulary

Find words or phrases in the passage which could be replaced by the following without changing the meaning of the passage.

Second paragraph:	(a)	restricted
Third paragraph:	(b)	sudden
	(c)	undamaged
Fourth paragraph:	(d)	disturbances of the earth's crust
Fifth paragraph:	(e)	broken to pieces
Sixth paragraph:	(f)	period
	(g)	strong
	(h)	ran away
	(i)	relatively quiet
	(j)	seen
Seventh paragraph:	(k)	disastrous
	(l)	thrown out
	(m)	fell in
	(n)	completely destroy
Eighth paragraph:	(o)	flood
	(p)	captured by

3: Technical vocabulary

Complete the following four definitions by inserting these terms:

CALDERA / TEPHRA / TSUNAMI / VOLCANIC CONE

You will have to use two of these terms twice.

(a) A _____ is a large, destructive ocean or sea wave caused by a violent disturbance of the earth's crust such as an earthquake or a volcanic explosion.

(b) _____ is relatively fine, dusty material that is forced out of a _____ by pressures inside the earth's crust.

(c) A _____ is a bowl-shaped hollow in a volcano after the top has been blown off by a violent volcanic explosion.

(d) A _____ is a regular-shaped hill formed by rocky materials (such as _____ and lava) being forced out of a hole in the earth's crust and building up around the hole.

4: Understanding

Arrange the following statements in the correct chronological sequence according to the volcanic theory, and supply a probable date or century for each:

1. The Minoan civilisation emerged.
2. The Minoan civilisation was destroyed.
3. The Thera volcano exploded, but without damage to human civilisation.
4. The Thera volcano exploded, causing tsunamis which destroyed cities on Crete.
5. The Thera volcano ejected a lot of tephra, which buried the Minoan settlements on the island at its rim.
6. The Mycenaeans captured Knossos.
7. The Minoan inhabitants of Thera left the island.
8. The findings of archaeological excavations on Thera were published.
9. The Minoan civilisation was rediscovered.
10. Thera was a volcanic cone.
11. Knossos was destroyed by an earthquake.

5: Transfer

Study the map below in relation to the text, and then complete the key:

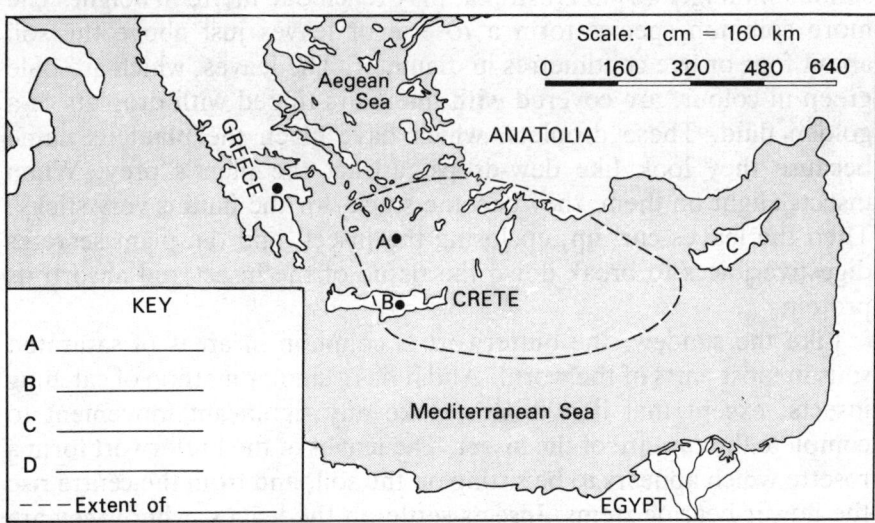

Library work

Find out about the Krakatoa eruption of 1883. What were its after-effects?

UNIT TWENTY-ONE

INSECTIVOROUS PLANTS

Plants feed by absorbing carbon dioxide from the air, and water and salts in solution from the soil through their roots. These substances from the soil are transformed into nourishment in the leaves by the action of sunlight and chlorophyll in the green cells. Thus, water,
5   minerals, carbon dioxide and light are essential to the life of every green plant, and plants have developed various ways of obtaining or preserving them in different conditions.

    One such uniquely adapted group of plants is that of the insectivorous, or insect-eating, plants. These plants do have green cells contain-
10   ing chlorophyll and therefore can produce their own nutrients, but the nitrogen they need comes from animal protein, which they obtain from insects. They have developed the means of attracting and trapping small insects and then digesting them. They are found mainly in marshy areas, where there is a relative shortage of nitrogen.

15   A very common insectivorous plant is the sundew, species of which can be found in very wet soils all over the world. The largest of the sundews, indigenous to Australia, may reach one metre in height. The more common species form a rosette of leaves just above the soil about four or five centimetres in diameter. The leaves, which are pale
20   green in colour, are covered with fine hairs tipped with droplets of a golden fluid. These droplets, which have given the plant its name because they look like dew-drops, attract the plant's prey. When insects alight on them, they become stuck, for the fluid is very sticky. Then the leaves curl up, enclosing the insect, and the plant secretes
25   digestive juices to break down the tissue of the insect and absorb its protein.

    Like the sundew, the butterwort is common in areas of saturated soils in most parts of the world. And it has a similar method of catching insects, except that it does not make any significant movement to
30   complete the capture of the insect. The leaves of the butterwort form a rosette which appears to be sitting on the soil, and from the centre rise the flower-bearing stems. Insects settle on the leaves, where they are trapped by the tiny hairs and the sticky surface. The edges of the leaf tend to curl over towards the insect, but this appears to play no part in
35   the actual capture.

A completely different type of insectivorous plant is found in the wet tropical regions around the Indian Ocean from Sri Lanka to the Malagasy Republic. This is the pitcher plant. It is so called because it is shaped like a pitcher, or jug: it has a vertical hollow body and an
40   opening at the top with a lip, opposite which is a lid on a short flexible stem. The insect enters the hollow chamber and slides down the smooth interior walls into a pool of digestive juices at the bottom. Here the insect's protein is extracted and absorbed by the plant.

Not all insectivorous plants live in the soil. The bladderwort, like the
45   sundew and the butterwort, is found in many parts of the world, but unlike these two it lives below the surface of the water. On its stem there are small green bladders, each of which has a trapdoor opening inwards. When a small water insect touches this, it opens slightly and the creature is carried inside by the resultant current of water. As soon
50   as the bladder is full of water, the trapdoor closes with the insect trapped inside.

One of the most famous insectivorous plants is restricted to one small area of the world, North and South Carolina in the United States. This is the venus fly trap. It has long leaves, at the end of which
55   are pairs of digestive glands surrounded by sensitive hairs. When these are touched, the glands fold together, the hairs curl up, and the hapless insect is trapped inside.

1: Reference

What do the following words refer to?
(a) they (line 11)
(b) them (line 13)
(c) them (line 23)
(d) they (line 23)
(e) it (line 28)
(f) this (line 34)
(g) Here (line 43)
(h) this (line 48)

2: Transfer

Insectivorous plants may be grouped functionally according to their trapping mechanisms.

In the pitfall type, the insect is lured into part of the plant and then it falls into a chamber containing a liquid from which it cannot escape.

The flypaper type is named after flypaper, which is a strip of paper covered with a sticky substance. An insect lands on the paper and sticks there until it is dead. The flypaper type of plants can be divided into two subtypes: the active and the passive. The active subtype attracts the insect on to a sticky surface and then closes around it, but the passive subtype simply attracts the insect and waits for it to die.

The steel-trap type of plant waits for an insect to land on its digestive pads and then snaps them shut like a trap operated by a steel spring.

The mousetrap type captures its prey by closing a trapdoor behind it after it has entered the digestive chamber.

Complete the following classification diagram by writing on the top line in each box the type (PITFALL, FLYPAPER, STEEL TRAP, MOUSETRAP, ACTIVE, and PASSIVE), and on the bottom line the name of an example of that type of plant.

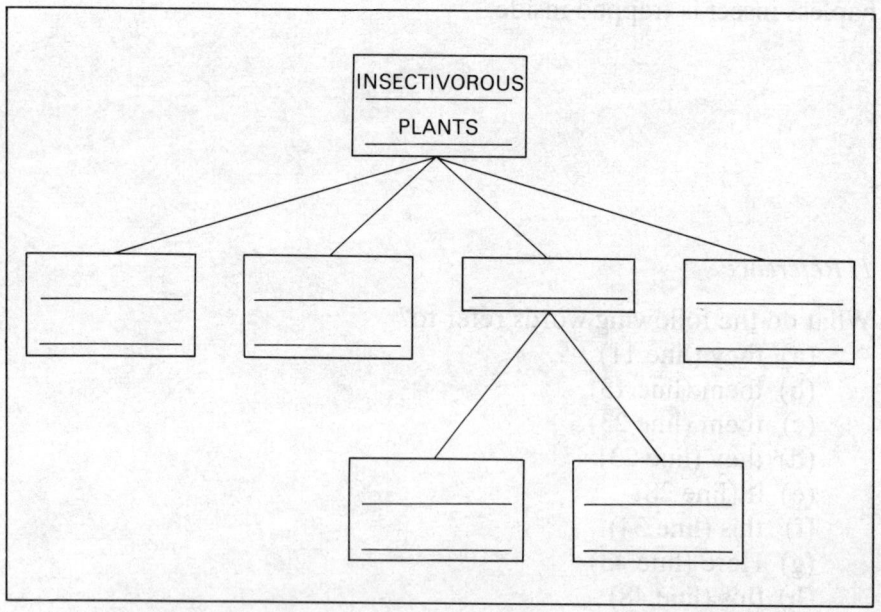

3: Transfer

Study the drawings of the plants labelled A to H. Five of them are described in the passage, and three are not. When you have decided which are which, complete the list below. Write X if a plant is not described.

A. _____

B. _____

C. _____

D. _____

E. _____

F. _____

G. _____

H. _____

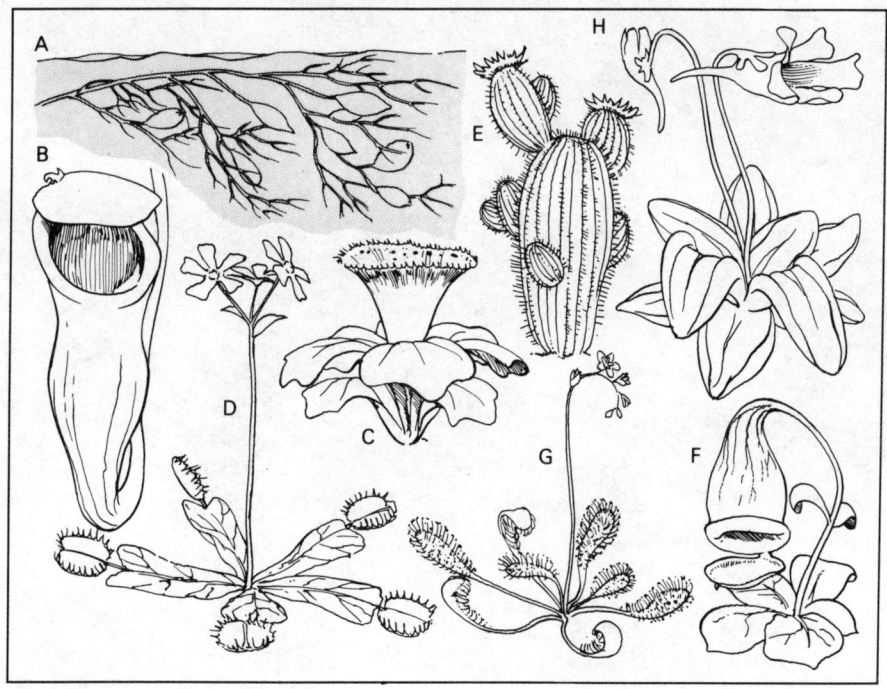

Library work

Find out (a) the botanical names of the plants described in this unit;

           (b) about the biochemical processes involved in the digestion of an insect by these plants.